PRAYER
OF THE
WARRIOR

Michael H. Brown

FAITH PUBLISHING COMPANY
P.O. BOX 237
MILFORD, OHIO 45150

Any reference contained in this book regarding current or past apparitions is presented with the knowledge that the final judgment
thereon rests with the Holy See of Rome, to whom the Publisher
willingly submits.

Published by: Faith Publishing Company
            P.O. Box 237
            Milford, OH 45150

For additional copies of this book, book dealers should contact the
publisher.

Individuals may request the book from:

The Riehle Foundation
P.O. Box 7
Milford, OH 45150

ISBN: 1-880033-10-0

Library of Congress Catalog Card No.: 93-072630

Cover design by Pete Massari

"Get thee hence, Satan!"
—Jesus

Table of Contents

For Lucia dos Santos,
true warrior in prayer,
truest of visionaries.

Acknowledgments

I would like to thank the literally thousands of people I've met in the last year, whose prayers and feedback have been so important. My special thanks to the Medjugorje centers across North America, who have so ably kept the spirit of Medjugorje alive, even during the Bosnian warfare. Father George Lukaczyk of Terryville, Connecticut, provided valuable background information on mystical theology, and Helen Sarcevic ably arranged my third trip to Medjugorje. My profoundest thanks to a select group of prayer-warriors across America who offered up their prayers and suffering for this project. May you all be specially blessed for helping a project so prone to spiritual attack and other forms of undermining or harassment. The enemy is behind our lines of defense; we find him everywhere. As always I also thank Bill and Fran Reck, my publishers/editors, for their capable and courageous handling of difficult material. Too, I thank their staffs at the Riehle Foundation and Faith Publishing for helpful input. I owe great thanks to Sister Nadine Brown and the Intercessors of the Lamb, a new community of nuns and hermits at Bellwether Queen of Peace, 4014 North Post Road, Omaha, Nebraska 68112; they specialize in discernment and spiritual warfare, worthy of all our support. My apologies to anyone I may offend in this blunt and candid book. I had to tell it like I saw it.

CHAPTER 1

A Spiritual War

We're in the midst of a war. It's not a political or cultural battle—though politics and culture are involved—nor is it a philosophical dispute. We humans, all of us, across the planet, are in the midst of a *spiritual* war. It's a war that has been brewing all our lives, in every nation, in every aspect of our lives, a battle between light and dark.

On one side are those who have taken the road toward God, who think in terms of Christ and an eternal destination; on the other side those who have fallen away from their faith and wittingly or unwittingly support the workings of an actual supernatural entity called Satan or Lucifer.

Right now it seems the dark is winning. Evil is rising as never before. We see it in the crime rate, in the divorce rate, in the rate of abortions. We see it when two 10-year-old children murder a baby in England, and we see it when a sinister Michigan doctor assists another "patient" in suicide.

We see it in the Bosnia-Hercegovina region of former Yugoslavia, where fierce tribalism among Serbians, Croatians, and Muslims has led to at least 130,000 dead and yet more thousands raped, starved, or tortured.

We see it in the flames of Waco, Texas, or in the blood-lust perpetrated by Hollywood. We see it in the guns which now accompany pen and notebook to school. We see it onstage with heavy-metal bands or in the unspeakable desires of Jeffrey Dahmer.

We see it on the face of a police officer in Olympia, Washington, who turns out to be a practicing Satanist and is arrested for sexually abusing his own daughters.

We see it in New York, where Saint John the Divine Episcopalian Church, the largest cathedral in America, displayed a bronze sculpting called "Christa"—a nude woman on a cross—one Holy Week and has allowed a New Age prophet to speak from the pulpit.

We see it in Colorado, where nuns pray to the rising sun and a priest wears a crystal.

We see it in Louisiana, where a famous evangelist is caught patronizing a prostitute.

We see it throughout our society, which has turned cold and hostile. Every day, each waking moment, evil finds its way into the news. We are all under its assault. It causes anxiety and depression. It causes division in our families. It plagues us with confusion and doubts. The war is waged on a supernatural stage, in the deepest recesses of our beings, and will overwhelm us if we don't do something about it.

When I left off in my book, *The Final Hour,* we were at the point where visionaries from around the world, especially at a site of reputed apparitions called Medjugorje (ironically in Bosnia-Hercegovina), were warning that the nefarious entity Satan is gaining momentum. It is the devil's "hour." It is his final hour of extended control. It is the hour of greatest spiritual difficulty and darkness. *"This is the time of the devil,"* says Our Lady of Medjugorje. *"The hour has come when the demon is authorized to act with all his force and power."*

All active Christians, whether Catholic or Protestant, are hearing similar words of knowledge. "If you look in any direction, whether it is technological or physiological, the world as we know it is coming to an end," laments preacher Billy Graham, while no less than former President Ronald Reagan has fretted that this generation may yet see Armageddon.

In Catholicism, which is my religious context, we have been told by prophets at places such as Fatima and LaSalette that these are conclusive times and that Satan, his time running out, is in the mood for a decisive battle. "It seems darkness is about to fall on the world," Pope Pius XII warned decades ago. "Humanity is in the grip of a supreme crisis."

Our mystics and demonologists say that this era was given to Satan as a special period of testing and though no one can be sure of God's time table, we all know our century is winding down to an uncertain conclusion.

Let me tell you straight from the shoulder: If we don't break down the evil, and soon, God may send forth trends and events, many unpleasant, perhaps cataclysmic, which will purge the evil for us. In my opinion this could begin with a simple withdrawal of His protective power, allowing not only continued demonic attack but also causing the physical world, which is but a shadow of the *spiritual* world, to fall away from equilibrium.

It is the force of God that keeps nature in balance, and if the Lord begins to withdraw His bonding force, we can expect a gradual increase, step-by-step, perhaps over an extended period, of both natural and man-made disasters.

Most will occur on a regional scale but may eventually be punctuated by a global event or a cosmic alarm.

I stress the words "gradual" and "regional." It could take years or decades for the momentum to build into a watershed occurrence. No one can say for sure. But we do know that through prayer and Christian action the momentum can be brought to a halt. I have no idea what to think of the terms "latter days" or "end times," which are included among some of the more spectacular prophecies mentioned in *The Final Hour*. We must remember that God's time is different from ours, and visionaries rarely have a good idea of *when* certain events will transpire. They are shown the extremes of various possibilities. It has been reported to me by Howard Q. Dee, former ambassador from the Philippines to the Vatican, that in a conversation with Joseph Cardinal Ratzinger, prefect of the Sacred Congregation for the Doctrine of the Faith, the cardinal hinted that there are essential similarities between messages from a supernatural episode in Akita, Japan, and the famous Third Secret of Fatima. At Akita, which has been formally approved in a pastoral letter from the bishop, Mary has warned that if it does not better itself shortly mankind will face a *"great chastise-*

ment" that will *"wipe out a great part of humanity."*

Akita also seems related to indications of forthcoming chastisement from Medjugorje, where six visionaries have been given secrets pertaining to the world.

The current era, a period of great and perhaps unprecedented evil, will conclude with either a whimper or a bang. It depends on us. I believe these secrets may relate more to a change of era than the "end times"—but a change of biblical proportions. While certain sections of *Revelation,* a living document that applies to every century, may be materializing before our eyes, I see our current situation more in terms of Nineveh or Sodom and Gomorrah. Whether or not we're in "end times," we are in extremely serious times, times that will bring forth grave events if our ways are not corrected in the near future.

Which is what this book is about: Satan and the spiritual war. I write about it from a personal perspective, for that is the easiest way of conveying the fashion in which Satan and his quislings afflict us. As such, the book you are about to read is rife with personal experiences. I belong to both the Marian and charismatic movements. Those of you who are non-Catholic are free to read or skip over the Catholic prayers, which are in italics. I admit to strong convictions, including the discernment that we must all prepare for the final stages of a battle which on a *spiritual* level does possess apocalyptical elements.

This is a book of my observations in the world of Christian mysticism, and I am only too well aware that mysticism is deep water. Just as non-Catholics have suffered their share of false prophets (and questionable televangelists), so too, do Catholics now struggle under the weight of false visionaries who knowingly or unknowingly are doing the devil's bid at creating further division and confusion. At one extreme are those who accept nothing supernatural (the "rationalists"); at the other extreme are those who do believe but may have fallen into the orbit of deceptive spirits. I am also well aware that apocalyptical proclivities are to be treated with great caution. From the Montanists of the second century to the dispensationalists of the 19th century, people have believed they were living in the days immediately preceding Christ's return. The pillaging of Rome by vandals in A.D. 410 was supposed to presage end times, as was the Black Death—bubonic plague—a thousand years later.

It's a natural inclination to anticipate huge moments at the end of a century, not to mention the end of a millennium. It is said that the last days of A.D. 999 were full of similar frenzy, the old Basilica of St. Peter packed with trembling worshipers who anticipated the end of the world. In the 14th century, during the great Western Schism, false seers rose everywhere and the holiest of men were given to dubious oracles. As long ago as the 12th century, one canonized saint was certain his generation would see arrival of the Anti-Christ and shortly afterward another saint announced that the Last Judgment was close.

We are always under the umbrella of God's Love, and we are recipients of great graces from the Holy Spirit. The joy is that God and the supernatural do exist and are ready to assist us. A great joy! We have come out of difficult periods before, and we will triumph with the Trinity. Great joy!

But something is different about our time. Something is especially diabolical about a time during which 37 million babies are killed each year and artists, funded with tax dollars, exhibit a photograph of Christ in a jar of urine. We must beware of creating a "doomsday" mentality, but we also must comprehend the enormity of current times on a spiritual level. Already we are in a period of supernatural chastisement during which demons are attacking with tremendous frequency and potency. This was prophesied in 1884 by Pope Leo XIII, who had a vision in which Satan was granted special powers for a century. In the end, Lucifer will be defeated. There is no doubting that. We are going to win. But if allowed to percolate much longer, this evil will materialize in economic and political events, including wars, famines, and societal chaos. There may also be astronomical or geophysical perturbations. I don't discount that at all. I will discuss the possibility of cataclysmic events and what may evolve into a great manifestation of Christ's power.

The end of the world, no, but a period of consternation, especially spiritual consternation: you bet.

My premise is simple. We are nearing a major change of era. The era that is coming will be glorious. It will mark the end of Satan's extended powers. That's why he is frantically lashing out. He wants to destroy as many souls as possible while he still has time. He wants to wreak carnage. He knows that the more evil there is in the world, the more God will have to send in the form of purification and chastisement.

If we don't break down Satan's power, and dispense with our own evil, the Lord will send forth trends and events which will purify His creation. He will do so out of love. He will wash the earth. The extent of devices available to Him are seen in the various prophecies. One way or another, the world is going to change, and it will experience such major change—a sociological sea change—within the lifetimes of the Medjugorje visionaries, who are now in their twenties. Currently we are headed into a final hour of darkness. It is an exceedingly dangerous time. Satan is pulling all stops. While I don't believe for a minute that we're facing the end of civilization, I *do* believe that, during the next several decades, we'll see truly major and perhaps unprecedented economic, military, sociological, theological, spiritual, and natural upheavals—if not sooner.

I'm not certain when or how the change will come about. We are told to discern the *"signs of the time"* (*Matt.* 16:3), and there is no greater sign than the current upsurge of evil and confusion. Indeed, the war with evil may already be manifesting in the physical world. During the past two years we've seen hostilities reach new and hideous heights in Bosnia-Hercegovina, we've seen terrible famine in Africa, we've seen proponents of abortion rise to power, and we've witnessed strange storms—storms of the century—in France, Hawaii, and New York.

A weird flood recently immobilized downtown Chicago, and there were tremors in Southern California—tremors and flash floods.

It was just after one especially severe quake that rioting broke out in Los Angeles.

Blood was also spilled in the former Soviet republics, which threaten to become a larger version of Bosnia.

Elsewhere a tidal wave lashed at Nicaragua, Hindus and Moslems clashed in India, a volcano haunted the Philippines, and the ocean threatened to inundate Guam—fulfilling visions of rising seas and unusual storms. Are these tiny little manifestations of spiritual conflict? Are these tiny little warnings of God's growing discomfort? Will those warnings gradually evolve into larger warnings, and then into global chastisement?

Off Long Island, beautiful homes floated in the Atlantic, washed from the beach fronts of Fire Island (which is famous as a homosexual community), while in California, center of Hollywood and occultism, mountainside abodes burned in brushfires or collapsed into mudslides and a river of water coursed through the tony streets of Beverly Hills.

Even *The New York Times* seemed to sense something with the weather. "Howling like Valkyries on a rampage, a huge prewinter storm packing gusts up to 90 miles an hour and enough rain to submerge a small state struck the New York metropolitan region today," noted the newspaper on December 11, 1992. "It crippled transportation, commerce, and education, flooded wide areas, knocked out power to hundreds of thousands of homes, damaged thousands of buildings, and disrupted the lives of millions of people."

That storm, with its bizarre sounds and fury, was described by commentators as the "storm of the century" until an even greater storm struck a few short months later, this time a blizzard which paralyzed the entire East Coast.

Elsewhere, torrents of rain in Sacramento. Snow in Birmingham. Floods in Arizona.

As always, as in biblical times, signs appear both in nature and in everyday society. Reports of car-jackings, child abuse, and AIDS are joined by reports of the destruction caused by Hurricane Andrew.

"In 1992 weird weather was everywhere," acknowledged a report over the Gannett News Service. "This past year saw some of the most extreme weather conditions on record, not only in the United States but around the world."

I can't prove that these are precursors or "pre-signs" but

it did seem like something was up. The year 1992 witnessed both the worst man-made disaster in American history—the rioting in Los Angeles—followed just a few short months later by one of the worst *natural* disasters in American annals—nearly $20 billion in damage caused by the Florida hurricane.

The events continued into 1993 as the United States came under the control of a new president whose very first acts were aimed at normalizing homosexuality and abortion.

As the year progressed, terrorism closed down the tallest skyscrapers in New York City, and the AIDS epidemic, caused mainly by drug use and perverted sex, turned all the more urgent.

In the Midwest, floodwaters from the Mississippi inundated much of the nation's very heartland, flooding that one meteorologist described as almost of "biblical proportions."

At the same time, quakes and tidal waves devastated Okushiri island in Japan while a tremor hit the Gulf of Patras in Greece.

Tiny little signals, these, but ones that may become more pronounced later in the decade. Perhaps we are entering the gradual beginning of portents that will slowly increase in intensity until we do indeed encounter an event or events of monolithic proportion. Signs of the times. Omens. People have watched for such signs throughout the ages. A comet appeared in the sky in 44 B.C., the year that Julius Caesar was assassinated, and Halley's Comet was seen in A.D. 66. That was just before Nero committed suicide and more importantly before the destruction of Jerusalem.

Those events were also accompanied by earthquakes from Crete to Judea, from Samos to Smyrna.

Around the same time, Mary, working her first known miracle, manifested herself to Saint James at Zaragossa.

When Halley's returned in 1531 (the year the Blessed Virgin Mary appeared in Guadalupe, Mexico), it was a period of tremendous, and at times violent spiritual turmoil.

Signs? Portents?

This much I know: A spiritual chastisement is already in progress. We are under demonic assault. Those who have opened their spiritual eyes recognize how the devil needles us, how he torments us, how he plants antagonistic, discouraging or morbid thoughts. More than anything, he sows division and confusion. Confusion is his hallmark. Confusion is the first sign that he is here. His confusion has plagued charismatics, Pentecostalists, and Evangelicals. It has plagued Catholics. He has confused the Marian movement as we try to sort through an unprecedented barrage of mystical reports.

Indeed, a spiritual chastisement is fully in progress and may soon be followed by chastisements in the physical realm.

That's what I want to focus upon: Our own state of spirituality and the personal trials we face as the battle heats up and possible chastisements loom. In God's army we'll win, but we have to know how to be prayer warriors, how to view the events around us, and how to purify ourselves. I want to take you on a more personal journey. I want to discuss *you,* your temptations, your fears, your difficulties, your struggles against dark forces as I share with you some of my own. This is a more personal book. It will offer a more personal look at certain saints and Church-approved visionaries, along with their insights into the world. It will offer glimpses of the afterlife. It will offer suggestions for spiritual protection. It is an account of both the good and evil I have witnessed as a journalist.

I am going to mention personal events which I never thought I would publicly discuss because the times necessitate such candor. We must lift our spiritual blinders and enhance our religious strength because in many ways America, a nation founded on Christian principles, has turned its back to God. We must all unite and realize that the world is dark and growing darker. It may be sunny where you're sitting now, but a great transcendental darkness is descending.

That shouldn't depress you. That shouldn't make you fearful. That shouldn't cause emotional upset. It should call you to action. It should call you to purification. It should excite you to the challenge and call you to the joys of greater individual spirituality.

Most of all, it should cause you to enlist in the army of the living God. He is alive. He wants to give us life more abundantly. He wants us to subdue the devil. That's the nature of earth: It is a constant struggle with darkness. Ten years ago I would have cast a bemused smile on anyone who wrote as I now write. I would have smiled with condescension. Lucifer! The devil! He was the stuff of fairy tales. He was just a symbol, an archetype that went back to the Stone Age. No rational adult actually believed in Satan, only "Jesus freaks" and other fanatics.

That was ten years ago, when I was still afflicted with spiritual hardness and blindness. That was before I was awakened by a series of experiences that may have been supernatural. As you can see, I am going to speak very frankly. I am not going to compromise with evil. I'm not "politically correct." I don't care what secular professors or Dr. Feelgoods think of me. I care about winning the war. I was once a secular writer who didn't believe in the devil but now I see his claws everywhere. Once I didn't give him a second thought, but now I see him besieging us, plaguing us with shock troops from Hell. The world is under his control as seldom before, and those of holiness now stand with Christ on the front lines, head to head with this infernal and soon to be vanquished foe.

CHAPTER 2

An Angel Named Michael

I returned to Christianity in the autumn of 1983, while I was living on the Upper East Side of Manhattan. I don't recall many details but I do know that a key element in my transformation was an exceedingly unusual dream. I have no idea if my interpretation is correct, nor can I prove it was supernatural or of God. Along with my other experiences, I'll leave that to your own judgment, or what is called discernment.

I can only give you my recollections. It was a Friday night, and I had been downtown socializing. I took a taxi home, went to bed, and as soon as I fell asleep I lapsed into a very vivid and peculiar dream. In it I was lying on a hospital gurney in the hall of my apartment, my feet toward the door.

I can still see much of it despite the passage of years. I was on that bed or gurney, and there were three of four luminous entities around me with their hands over me, as if healing me. I wasn't able to look directly at them—I saw no face—but it seemed like they were very thin and other-worldly, certainly not human but probably able to assume human form.

It seemed to me that they were communicating among themselves. I couldn't make out any words. They seemed benevolent, yet firm and authoritative.

11

They were healing me and I addressed the one closest to the left side of my head. He seemed to be in charge. "Who are you?" I asked. I may have asked the question more than once before getting an answer.

"My name is Michael," he finally said. "Now look."

The dreamlike entity raised his arm or somehow indicated toward the apartment door. There on the white door, where the peephole and doorbell box were located, materialized a very detailed, elongated, and *awful* face. I could never hope to write an adequate description. There was a hideous and terrifying quality to this face that defies characterization. The long face was hollowed at the cheeks, rather smirking, with a pointy goatee and deepset eyes, a gray but living image, sketched and disembodied but very *alive.*

Instantly I woke up. I was alarmed. I was scared. Though the face was not technically ugly—no horns, no scaly skin, no red eyes—there was something about it that I found terrifying beyond adjectives. I'd never seen anything like it, not even in horror movies. No human could have duplicated its evil quality. I knew instinctively and immediately that it was the face of Lucifer.

I got out of bed, padded to the living room, and sat on the couch, contemplating what I had just encountered in this strange dream, this dream that was wholly unlike any night-time vision I had ever previously experienced. For the next twenty to thirty minutes, as best I can remember, I sat mulling it over. There was the strong sensation that I was being shown something. There was the sensation that I was being warned about something in my life.

My life? It was the fast lane. I was a young freelance writer, under contract at the time with Simon & Schuster, finishing a book about the Mafia. It was what I'd always wanted: travel all the time, challenging interviews, tricky research, exciting journalism. If it got lonely on occasion, because I had not yet married, not to worry, there were attractive women all over New York. Every night: the cafes, restaurants, and bars. Looking for Miss Goodbar. In fact that Friday I had been out with two women I knew from the Chelsea area who lived in a townhouse that they claimed was "haunted."

I sat on the sofa, smoking a cigarette and thinking. I thought about my long-held interest in haunted houses and parapsychology, or "psychic phenomena." I thought about the two young women, one of whom worked for a major publisher, and how they often regaled me with stories about strange noises in their townhouse, inexplicable odors, and objects moving of their own accord—a window that opened and closed by itself.

I forget if we talked about the house that night, before I took my taxi home. Probably not. There were other things we discussed. But it was like something had rubbed off. I thought about the dream and its preternatural quality. I mulled it over a while longer but it didn't take too much to get back to sleep. It was just a dream, right? The image of the devil had worn off.

But as soon as I fell asleep I lapsed back into the very same dream. It was a two-part dream. I had never had one of those before.

And it had such an odd quality. It didn't seem like it was really a dream. It seemed more like a vision.

Very vivid.

I was on the gurney again, in the front hall, feet toward the door, kitchenette to my left, a wicker mirror to my right. The luminous entities once more had their hands over me, and they were probably in prayer. They were certainly meditating. Baffled, I remained perfectly still. I felt no sensations good or bad and kept moving my head from side to side. I have no idea how long these dreams lasted.

After a while the one who said his name was "Michael" again addressed me. "Look," he repeated, pointing again toward the door, in a very muscular voice. "Now, say 'Vanish!'"

The long, line-drawn, awful face of the devil, human and yet not really human, appeared again on the door. It was like a black-and-white sketching and yet so *alive,* staring right at me.

I didn't have the courage to say "Vanish." I had the strength only to wake up again. This time I was up for much longer—close to an hour—and believe me, I was *terrified.*

Pacing. From the bedroom to the bathroom to the

kitchenette and across the parquet floor of the living room, pacing and looking out toward Lexington Avenue and beyond that Central Park, and downtown to the angular Citicorp skyscraper and the Chrysler Building.

Terrified and in need of company. Night-time in Manhattan. A lonely time. It was probably four or five in the morning. The last of the stragglers had left the bars lining Third Avenue, and now there was only the occasional swish of a racing cab and the far-off echo of a siren heading toward Harlem.

Here I was in America's most densely populated city, more than 24,000 people per square mile, several hundred living in my own apartment building, and I'd never felt so apprehensive and alone. That face. That awful unforgettable face. Sneering at me. At my door.

I was frightened in the true sense of the word. No: I was *terrified.* I had never been so scared. The face in the dream, the face of the devil, had a power that was far beyond my previous experience. The potency went beyond its mere image. It had been so real and *living.*

I thought about calling someone, but who was I going to wake up at four or five in the morning? At the time my two closest friends in Manhattan were a couple on the West Side, both of whom had worked as reporters for *The New York Times.* Reporters for *The New York Times* didn't believe in the supernatural. They certainly didn't believe in the devil. What was I going to do, call them in the middle of the night to say that the devil was appearing on my door?

I'm sure I smoked a couple more cigarettes and then, after about an hour, was able to put myself back to bed and drift off.

As soon as I did the dream continued right where it had left off. I was on that gurney again and the entities were around me praying. They didn't have wings, but I had the distinct impression that they were entities from Heaven or *somewhere* out there—maybe angels.

The one who had identified himself as "Michael" addressed me again. I can't remember all that he told me. It's somewhere deep in my subconscious. But I do remember him saying again, "I told you, say *'Vanish!'*"

Again the awful face appeared on the door. Again I found it potent and horrifying. But now I had a strange inner strength. I summoned all the courage I had, raised my hand, and shouted, "VANISH!"

Instantly the face of the devil disappeared. It was no longer on the door. Instead, there was now a ring of keys hanging on a peg, with an address tag. The entities or angels were also gone, and in the dream I got up, took the keys, looked at the address tag, and on it was the address of the "haunted" townhouse in which those women I knew lived.

I'll get back to that in a moment. But first let me tell you what happened afterward. It may have been the very next day. It's hard to remember. What I do know is that it was very soon afterward. I decided to visit my twin sister, Maureen, who lives north of New York in Stamford, Connecticut. I took the Number Six subway to Grand Central and boarded a Metro North train for Connecticut, seeking refuge in her condominium after all I was going through.

My mother had been visiting her recently, helping with a newborn baby girl, and my sister told me that mom had left something for me before returning to Niagara Falls, which is where the rest of my family lives. A gift. Without saying what it was Maureen went upstairs and came down with a beautiful plaster statue that was about two feet high, the statue of a young winged angel with a silver breastplate and a sword that was thrust into the mouth of a dark brown serpent. I knew immediately that it was a statue of the Archangel Michael.

CHAPTER 3

A Brush With the Mafia

I don't really know what it meant, but certain things about that dream will become clearer as we go on. It was important on several levels. First and foremost, it was part of my conversion. I was born and raised a Catholic, in a fairly devout family, but hadn't been a regular churchgoer for well over a dozen years.

That was the first effect: the dream helped propel me back into the pews. Suddenly I found myself at Our Lady of Good Counsel Church, just half a block down 90th Street, sitting through Mass and using holy water.

In short order I began attending daily Mass. I became what they call a daily communicant.

I was amazed at the relief, the refreshment and strength, I felt upon dabbing my forehead with holy water.

I never believed it had actual power.

Now I *felt* it.

And that was nothing compared to the grace and peace that flowed from the top of my head to the bottom of my feet when I received the Eucharist.

It had been so long since I'd attended Mass that I had to relearn the rituals and brush up on the changes which had been instituted since I was a youngster. For one thing, the only Creed I knew was the longer version, and last time

16

I could remember they said three "Lord I am not worthys" just before Communion—not the one I now heard. Back in Niagara Falls, when last I had attended Mass, there in my hometown, before college, they still knelt at the altar rail for Communion. Now, I noticed, everyone lined up in a nearly informal fashion and took Communion in the palms of their hands.

I watched the other congregants so I knew when to stand and when to kneel. I was afraid of making a fool of myself. I felt out of place and nervous—like Protestants or Jews who visit a Catholic Mass probably feel.

Here I was, a young man having to relearn my faith and the basic tenets of Christianity. Here I was, having to acquaint myself with the rich traditions even though as a youngster I had been taken to Mass every day during Lent by my grandmother and had grown up with scapulars, medals of Saint Michael, and a statue of St. Thérèse of Lisieux in my room.

Here I was a 31-year-old who really wasn't sure of the difference between the Old and New Testaments—who didn't even know what the word "fornication" meant—even though I had attended a Jesuit college.

Despite my parents' devotion, and their steadfast adherence to Church strictures, including Friday fasts, I had stopped being a Catholic during high school and especially during my years at Fordham University. Religion had ceased to factor into my vocabulary. I never knew the religious orientation of women I dated. We never talked about anything like that. I thought organized religion was all archaic and empty ritual. I didn't really believe there could be power in a wafer of bread. I thought Mass was a relic from a previous era—before mankind was enlightened by science and rationalism.

I did think there were undiscovered "energies" in the universe, such as powers of the mind, and that religion might have been an ancient way of understanding those energies. In fact for many years I had a side interest in ESP, and had written an article about experiments that tested for the ability of people to affect thermal-noise or nuclear random-event generators. I'd written about them for *Reader's Digest* and

The Atlantic Monthly. I'd also once written about a "psychic"
back when I was a newspaper reporter.
  God?
  I never ceased to believe in a Supreme Being.
  But He was someone or something way out there.
  It was not an active faith.

  My personal life?
  I was a product of the "sexual revolution." I had no conception of wrong or right, and neither did the women I
dated.
  The word "sin" had also disappeared from our enlightened vocabularies.

  But suddenly, miraculously, I was back. I was back to
being a Christian. Not only that, but attending daily
Mass—a daily communicant. That's how powerful the
dream was. That's how powerful were other things I began
encountering. The dream had come in the midst of a very
trying time for me. I didn't know it back them, but during
the late summer and autumn of 1983 I was under full-
fledged demonic assault. Everything was going wrong. I
was struggling with a magazine assignment, and I just
knew it wasn't going to work, despite the $25,000 I had
been offered for that article.
  It was to be an adaptation of the Mafia book, and I had
five or six weeks to do it, but I knew the article wasn't
going to pan out. I was just miserable, physically and mentally. I remember feeling as if something were throwing
mud—balls of mud—at my livingroom windows. It was an
incredible sensation: I felt harassed every waking moment
and often during sleep. I didn't know *what* it could be.
Something was suddenly around. It was making every waking minute miserable. At one point, in my bathroom,
plagued with a nearly uncontrollable diarrhea, I actually
thought I heard a sinister voice laughing at me.

  To this day I don't know exactly what brought it all on.
I do know it was spiritual harassment, and looking back,
it could have been caused by any number of things that
were going on in my life. Maybe it was my Mafia book,
Marked To Die, the story of a former New Jersey gangster

who, along with his beleaguered family, was hiding from the mob. He had been caught in a murder conspiracy and in return for clemency agreed to testify against something like 74 thieves, hoodlums, and hitmen from Newark and surrounding areas.

When I met this gangster, whose nickname was "Chicken Delight," his hideout was along the East Coast, near the Chesapeake Bay. I spent many weeks there interviewing him, and maybe the grime around him—he was definitely no choir boy—had somehow rubbed off on me.

There was a quality about this man, an inner quality, that I couldn't define at the time but was often repulsive and galling. The first weekend at his "hideout" I had to stop him from smacking his wife across the face with a revolver. He was in one of his nasty moods, depressed and drunk. A violent guy. Around 6-foot-6. With a huge blockish face that reminded me of Lurch. While he wasn't what cops and FBI agents call a "stone-cold" killer, he was violent enough for my tastes, and virtually all of his closest cronies had been implicated in mob murders. They were part of a crew that did "hits" for the biggest mob bosses in America, including Carlo Gambino of New York City, who was *capo di tutti capi,* boss of bosses, in the American Mafia.

I had interviewed a few of these killers, and as the spiritual harassment continued I had wondered: did something jump like a flea from those hoodlums and latch on to me? Did they cast a shadow on me? One of Chicken Delight's old cronies was an assassin known as "The Bear," and another was a nearly zany but exquisitely treacherous bank robber who was now being held in a penitentiary north of Houston.

The fellow in Texas was an especially stone-cold killer. I'll never forget flying to Houston and driving north a couple hours to the sprawling maximum-security prison in Lovelady. As soon as the guards brought him into the visiting pen I could feel his presence. He had an incredible air about him—a very perilous charisma—and one fairly high-ranking FBI agent in Washington, D.C., Michael Wilson, later told me this gangster was one of the most dangerous criminals with whom the agency had ever dealt. His eyes were so incredible—bulging, cold, and gelid—that we used to joke he could have intimidated Charles Manson.

It wasn't far from the truth. This man had probably killed fifteen to twenty people in the course of his career (he referred to murder as "a piece of work"), and he was also widely known not only as a bank robber but as a major arsonist, heroin trafficker, and jewel thief. He even sold babies that had been born to prostitutes. In Houston, where he was operating incognito thanks to the Witness Protection Program, he became a big-time fence and pimp, running seedy massage parlors.

Around the time of my dream I had returned to Texas to share information with another federal agent, Randy Cunningham of ATF (the Bureau of Alcohol, Tobacco, and Firearms), who was pursuing the gangster and had some interesting conversations that he had taped while undercover with the hoodlum. We talked about the Jersey hoodlum, and we also talked about something else: *evil.* I asked if he believed in actual evil. I mentioned the extraordinary presence—the awful presence—that accompanied the gangster, and he earnestly agreed. He'd felt the same intangible peril. Even then, before my formal conversion, I had started wondering about the existence of evil because of what I felt around these hoodlums or saw in their mugshots, especially their *eyes.* Looking into their pupils one sensed an inexplicable iciness and sometimes even a tension bordering on nausea. There was something cold and reptilian behind their pupils. There was something beyond simple criminality. Something awful and glazed and inhuman. I remembered how in Maryland the gangster's children complained of strange happenings in the hideout—what a parapsychologist would call "poltergeist" phenomena—in the way of small objects winging across his daughter's bedroom and a strange force that seemed to take over this girl, who was known to fall into a trance and act like she needed an exorcist.

As a journalist you see many things, you're much more exposed to various elements than the average person. It's your duty to walk onto unfamiliar terrain. Gangsters. Haunted houses. To me it wasn't something frightening, it was just *interesting.* You have to remember, at the time I still wasn't convinced of the existence of metaphysical evil. I thought "evil" was something biochemical or psychological. The word did not really mean that much to me. It was a generic term. It meant things or events or people who were negative and anti-social, perhaps psychopathic. It meant negative events like crime or war, some form of disaster.

But now I was beginning to wonder if evil was an actual force. Why the trances and poltergeist phenomena? What was the almost tangible force emanating from the mugshots?

"Evil." Death. Destruction. These were hitmen. These were destroyers of lives. Was it a coincidence, I now wondered, that "evil" is the word "live" spelled backwards?

Today I recognize how very evil the situation was. I myself thought I was doing good, exposing organized crime, and at the hideout I had often counseled the mobster's children, urging them to study and helping to prevent one from having an abortion when she became pregnant at the age of 16. I wasn't a *bad* person. I even put quotes in the Mafia book that had spiritual meaning.

But my own household needed to be put into order, and I was simply around too much evil. There was something threatening everywhere I turned, and I couldn't put my finger on it. The word "evil" hadn't really been a part of my vocabulary. And the term "devil" certainly wasn't.

But after the dream, after the face on my door, it was on my mind quite a bit.

The devil. Lucifer. Old Beelzebub.

I felt the dream was telling me that he was too close for comfort.

CHAPTER 4

The House in Chelsea

I began reviewing my life, not only the personal mistakes I'd made, not only my spiritual negligence, not only the Mafia project, but happenings in my life that were related to the supernatural. No doubt I was exposed to evil on the cop-and-robber beat, but I knew it was something more. I knew there were other reasons.

In the dream I was shown that ring of keys, and on the ring of keys was the address of the "haunted" townhouse occupied by those women I knew and located on West 21 Street, in the area of Manhattan known as "Chelsea."

The spiritual attack seemed linked to the house, which was inhabited by several people. Three of the current or past residents worked in the publishing business, another was a science-fiction novelist, and there had also been a holistic "healer."

It wasn't like we were best of friends—my closest buddies were cops, newsmen, and brokers on Wall Street—but on occasion I would visit the women who lived in the townhouse and for a while I dated one. We had a common interest: psychic phenomena. All my life I had been fascinated by accounts of ghosts and telepathy. So if the Mafia wasn't enough, I got my full quotient of danger by nosing around haunted houses and occasionally socializing with people who were interested in what I now call the occult

22

but which I used to think of as science of the mind or "parapsychology."

I didn't think of it as "the occult" because it didn't involve black magic or spells. I certainly didn't see it as evil. To me it was an exciting new field of research, and I was looking for proof, objective proof, of the supernatural. I lacked faith. I was starving spiritually.

This unhealthy interest came about for several reasons. All my life I had encountered mystical experiences. When I was young they were more of a religious nature, but with age my mystical bent was diverted into more "scientific" approaches to the supernatural. I was searching. During college I had gone through a crisis of doubt—agnostic, wondering if there was really an afterlife—and I was searching for concrete evidence. If psychic phenomena and ghosts existed, I figured, then there might be an afterlife after all. ESP indicated the existence of something outside the body, something *immaterial.*

I wanted laboratory evidence of the soul. I wanted concrete proof of "spirits." My head was filled with the rationalism of science and the convoluted philosophy that was shoved down our throats in college. If the supernatural existed, I wanted evidence; I wanted something I could touch or *see.*

Which is where psychic phenomena and haunted houses came in. If there was really a soul, if the mind of man went beyond the physical body, if we live after death, there would be evidence in the new science of parapsychology.

And this townhouse in Manhattan: it seemed like an active case. It seemed like it was inhabited by "spirits." The residents all told me about objects that would move by themselves or the window up in the front bedroom on the second floor, which they claimed would sometimes open and shut by itself, before their astounded eyes. That's what I wanted: something I could see!

It was spooky. It sent a titillating jolt up my spine. This place really did seem haunted. The people who lived there were intelligent and sophisticated, not the type who fabricated stories or were easily scared. True, they were believers in paranormal phenomena, but they were also realists. They told me of magazines or books on the coffee table that opened and closed without a draft or any other visible reason.

There were also noises in the dark of night. And the cat seemed to see something.

Who was the ghost? Was it someone who had lived there?

That's what I thought haunted houses are all about: spirits of the dead returning. In some cases they probably are, but I didn't consider the other possibility: demons. Before moving to New York I had investigated a number of similar hauntings in Niagara Falls and Binghamton. I'll relate some of those accounts later. Spirits of the dead. In most hauntings, it seemed someone had died in the house or the spirit was related to one of the residents.

In the Chelsea townhouse there were indications that it was a poltergeist or troublesome "ghost." The word "poltergeist" was coined in Germany during the Reformation and means noisy spirit. I knew that back in olden times, back before mankind had become "enlightened," those who were the centers of poltergeist activity were cast away as malefic wizards and witches. How childish, I thought. How ridiculous to ascribe such happenings to imps and demons. True, poltergeist phenomena often preceded cases of demonic possession, but I had interviewed a prominent parapsychologist in Toronto, Dr. A.R.G. Owen, who'd taught biology and math at Trinity College in Cambridge, and he had assured me that poltergeists are just cases of subconscious psychic power—that the phenomena are due to energy coming from living people, not spirits. Dr. Owen had personally investigated a famous poltergeist case that began on November 22, 1960, in Sauchie, Scotland, and it was similar to what I was now hearing at the Chelsea townhouse: the case started with loud, angry knockings and supposedly ended up with bedroom furniture tilting upward or actually levitating.

But there was something about the Manhattan townhouse that seemed to go beyond psychic energy. There was something sinister about it. There was something that seemed suffocating and dark. There was something that seemed independent of humans. The women claimed that when they brought in a Christmas tree it lost its needles the very next day, and that plants would die instantaneously and mysteriously upon placement in the living room.

That wasn't all. There were those foul odors in the house, and the cat that seemed terrified of something. I remember one of the women calling me in a panic because she was alone and could hear footsteps. They were following close behind her.

When this woman moved to an apartment it seemed to follow her; one winter day she came home to find a swarm of flies covering part of a wall.

I knew only too well that there aren't any flies during cold weather in New York, certainly not enough to swarm on a wall.

I'll never know the answers. The last time I ever socialized with anyone from that house was the night of my dream. I never went back. Something was too close for comfort. I couldn't figure it out, but it was like one thing led to another and I wanted nothing to do with either. Haunted houses. The Mafia. They seemed disconnected and yet inexplicably linked.

What in the world did the Mafia have in common with a townhouse full of people in the publishing business?

Why was there something about one of the women who lived there, something in her attitude and eyes, that reminded me of the gangster down in Texas?

I found out later that this one particular woman, who worked in a publisher's publicity department and had joined us socially that Friday night, worshiped secretly in a closet in the bedroom of that townhouse, the bedroom with the moving window, and believe me, it wasn't any Christian ritual.

CHAPTER 5

The Bells of Good Counsel

As I will throughout, let me lead a little prayer here, so that we stay on top of things.

> *"Lord Jesus, cleanse us of all evil. Wash us of all spiritual grit. Let us all learn from my experiences, and from our own experiences. Let us review certain aspects of evil but without becoming enticed or obsessed by them. Let this be for all an experience of the Holy Spirit and of His sure deliverance."*

Grit. That's what evil feels like. Tension and grit.

All of us are exposed to it, but usually it's at a level less intense than what is encountered by a nosy journalist.

Between those spooks in Chelsea and the Newark mob, I was lucky to get out of it without a major disaster. Not lucky, *blessed.* I know that during all those years my parents and grandparents were praying for me.

Years later I found out that my grandmother had a special devotion to Our Lady of Good Counsel—which is also the name of the church where I sought protection and deliverance!

I'll never forget that place, half a block from my apartment, at 230 East 90th Street. In a smaller city, Good

Counsel would have been considered a cathedral. It was not only high and broad but built with exquisite craftsmanship. Its broad facade was intricately carved granite that reached upward about six or seven stories, fringed with dormers and flanked by Gothic towers.

A couple stories up, between the two front entrances, was an encased white Madonna. She was watching the street.

She had probably watched any number of times as I rollicked by on the way to restaurants like Rathbones or Elaine's on Second Avenue—oblivious to her and the church, which I hadn't even really noticed before my conversion. I had hardly realized that monolith was there!

Because it is set on a sidestreet among buildings that are also tall, you could walk right by Our Lady of Good Counsel without really *seeing* it. It blends into the city, the front close to the sidewalk, just another chunk of the great urban wall.

But viewed from across the street it is fairly breathtaking. It's a true masterpiece of design, and as I recall, the stones had been imported from Europe.

Our Lady of Good Counsel was named after an Italian basilica which was located at the site of a miracle southeast of Rome in the town of Genazzano. A picture of Mary had miraculously materialized at the site of the basilica back in the 15th century. It was near the ancient ruins of a pagan temple. As she had at Guadalupe in Mexico, Mary arrived in Italy to replace pagan idolatry (the temple was devoted to the love goddess Venus) with Christian veneration.

The Virgin of Good Counsel had shoved aside the goddess of lust, and as at Guadalupe, her eyes were cast downward, in a pensive mood.

To me it wasn't just a church but a fort and refuge. I would hear the bells at noon and rush out my door down the elevator and past the doorman for Mass. Most of the time there were just a handful of us, and I was the only one under the age of sixty, sitting there amid the sweet white-haired women with fraying sweaters and Irish brogues. Usually I sat in the right wing, near the statue of a saint who became very important to me, Saint Joseph.

As I said, it was a fort, and that's just what I needed.

I was under attack. For whatever reason—or *reasons,* plural
—the devil was openly showing himself. He was on the
attack, and God was granting me the grace to see it and
do something about it.

No doubt some of the problems came from the rugged
business of journalism. I had my share of enemies. Before
venturing into the project on organized crime, I had written
a major book and dozens of newspaper and national magazine stories exposing the problem of toxic wastes across
America.

A number of corporations, including some of the largest
in America, weren't especially happy with me.

One of them had enlisted the nation's leading libel attor-
ney, Louis Nizer, to try and stop my book, *Laying Waste:
The Poisoning of America by Toxic Chemicals* (Pantheon
and Pocketbooks), from coming out.

I found myself in heated confrontations with executives
whose PCBs or dioxin were contaminating homes, waterways, or drinking wells.

Any number of companies were involved, and they
didn't take kindly to such exposure. We battled on radio
programs, local TV, and national broadcasts such as *Nightline* and *The Today Show.*

I'd seen some awful cases around the country, kids born
with birth defects, and I was upset about it.

A photographer took pictures to go along with an article I
wrote for *The New York Times Magazine,* and one of them
was of a goose born in Michigan with its wings on backward.

That project, chemical wastes, had begun in 1978 and
1979 when I was a reporter unearthing the first evidence
of a health threat—not just environmental problems, which
were already known, but an actual health threat—next to
the chemical dump that soon became infamous as "Love
Canal." People there were complaining about an assort-
ment of ailments.

I had taken a little survey of health problems, an informal
study of one neighborhood, and began communicating
with the staff of Dr. David Axelrod, who soon became New
York State Health Commissioner.

Dr. Axelrod was equally concerned, and state techni-
cians conducted a medical investigation that found an

abnormal rate of birth defects and miscarriages in the most contaminated part of the neighborhood. Meanwhile I learned, by having a few water samples tested at a local laboratory and by reviewing internal company documents, that the Love Canal was two or three times the size everyone figured; that the chemicals may have crossed bordering streets, threatening many more people; and that the chemical company had dumped dioxin, a compound that was supposed to be about as toxic as chemicals get. Eventually more than 1,000 families were relocated.

From Love Canal I had gone on to uncover other potentially hazardous dumps, including one that was adjacent to the drinking-water plant for the city of Niagara Falls and others, owned by various outfits, that were leaking into Lake Ontario, the source of water for millions downstream, including the city of Toronto.

When *Laying Waste* came out, it received large reviews in publications such as *The New York Times, The Washington Post* and *Newsweek,* creating somewhat of a firestorm. I did many dozens of TV and radio shows. Love Canal had started a new health issue, and President Jimmy Carter signed into law a "superfund" to stop similar pollution across the nation.

I mention this because in 1983 I began thinking back to other times I had encountered the tense and gritty sensation. I'd felt it during Love Canal, and I'd also felt something ominous along a tremendously contaminated bayou in Baton Rouge, Louisiana (which, interestingly enough, was known as "Devil's Swamp").

A lot of harassment was directed my way during the toxic-waste project, political and spiritual harassment, along with professional jealousies that deeply hurt; it had been an excruciatingly difficult and yet exhilarating battle. Was I still suffering a hangover from the war with polluters?

And was I also suffering a spiritual malaise from the time when I was a cub reporter doing that article I mentioned on psychic phenomena?

No doubt. Without knowing it, I had been under spiritual attack. Michael must have been watching out for me all along. Michael was my patron, he was the archangel who threw Satan out of Heaven, and he was showing me that, along with everything else, my unhealthy interest in parapsychology, which we now call "New Age," as well as my battles with chemical companies and my brushes with mob types, without adequate spiritual armor, had brought the devil to my doorstep.

He was also showing me that I could make the devil vanish if I had courage and faith.

If you recall, when I finally summoned the fortitude to say "Vanish!" the devil disappeared.

"VANISH!"

In the wake of the dream and conversion, in the wake of increasing harassment, I quickly learned that demons actually exist in countless numbers and that they are around every one of us, interacting with humans constantly.

I could feel their rage when I brought the statue of the Archangel Michael into my home.

I could feel their struggle to keep me away from Jesus.

In one dream it was like an explosion had ripped the plaster from my apartment walls.

The deeper I prayed the more those demons raged. I was tormented with anxiety. I felt oppressed and lonely. At one point my heart squeezed tight and felt like there were claws digging into it.

These were all tactics, I realize now, to try and scare me away from prayer. I have no doubt about that. Satan's assaults were fierce, causing me great emotional strain, but at the same time I was experiencing the greatest joys of my life, moments of immense bliss and jubilation.

I could taste the grace in my mouth after Mass and praying the Rosary.

Yes, I quickly relearned the Rosary. To my surprise I discovered that my mother had left an old black rosary with a Saint Anne Beaupre medal in a corner of my chest of drawers. My dear mother who'd also given me the Michael statue!

I know those of you who are not Catholic have problems with the Rosary. Let me take a moment to mention a few things. The first is that praying the Rosary is a meditation on the life of Jesus. We meditate on 15 "mysteries" of His life and that of His mother. It includes the *Lord's Prayer*, which is simply a recitation of the way Jesus Himself told us to pray (*Matthew* 6:9-13), and the *Gloria*—a prayer to the Trinity: *"Glory be to the Father, to the Son, and to the Holy Spirit."* As for the *Hail Mary*, it is largely a set of quotations from Elizabeth and the Angel Gabriel, which are documented in *Luke* (26-28). The *Hail Mary* may date back, in some form, to Saint James of Antioch and Saint Mark of Alexandria, and that would bring us as far back as the fifth or even the fourth centuries.

"Hail Mary, full of grace, the Lord is with thee. Blessed art thou among women, and blessed is the fruit of thy womb, Jesus."

What grace! What power in those words! What protection! It is a request for Mary to pray for us, just as we ask others to pray for us. Except that the Virgin is in a better position than anyone I know to pray to Jesus.

"Pray for us sinners, now and at the hour of our death . . ."

When I was under attack, the attack would immediately dissipate—the gritty tension would flee—after recitation of the Rosary. I've read accounts from demonologists who have learned the efficacy of the Virgin during deliverance. "At an exorcism on the 14th of February, 1879, the demon of the possessed was humiliated, and on quivering knees pointed out the presence of the Savior and the Blessed Virgin to us," recalled an Italian exorcist in his memoirs. "The fear of the demon was most intense."

During another exorcism a demon complained that Mary "is altogether kind and merciful toward you, but for us she is a torture."

I wanted anything the demons *didn't* want, and the Rosary, along with prayers invoking Michael and the angels, and most importantly praises to Jesus, ended many spiritual attacks. To my amazement I felt the flow of an ineffable grace. A delicious peace. It was like a cool glass of water on a scorching desert. No matter how fiercely I was being assaulted, I could lie down, and if I spent enough time with the Rosary or reading Scripture, the demonic attack would lift and anxiety would be replaced with peace, comfort and warmth.

Oh, sometimes it took *several* Rosaries. It wasn't like a tablespoon of medicine. Sometimes I had to stick with it for an hour or better, and still the attack would linger.

But most of the time, prayer and reading the Bible brought nearly immediate relief.

The devil hates the Bible, and he hates the Rosary. Those two lessons I learned immediately.

Thumbing through books at a Christian bookstore near Lexington Avenue, I came across a little blue and white book of the Scriptural Rosary. It had a biblical reading for every bead of the 15 decades. I can't tell you how powerful it was. If an attack was especially bad, I would set myself down and say the entire 15 decades without stop. The attack would often dissipate like a morning fog. What grace. What a defense.

I had never been to a prayer group, so I didn't pray the Rosary like many did. It wasn't as formal, and I didn't have strict meditations when I used the beads. The important thing was to say *"Our Fathers"* and *"Hail Marys"* and *"Glory Bes"* often and with feeling. I started praying throughout the day, whenever I wasn't at the computer writing or on the phone. I prayed taking a shower and in the kitchenette and in the elevator. I prayed up and down Third Avenue.

I became spirit-filled and couldn't get enough of Christ and His mother. Later, I'll mention how I prayed with non-Catholics, and what I learned with them. But my initial conversion, the way I was "born again," was through the angels and saints. I picked up devotional pamphlets. I started novenas to Saint Jude and Thérèse the Little Flower. And I said the prayer asking assistance from the Archangel Michael:

> *"Saint Michael the Archangel, defend us in battle, be our safeguard against the wickedness and snares of the enemy. May God rebuke him, we humbly pray, and do thou, oh prince of the heavenly Host, by the power of God, cast into Hell Satan and all the evil spirits who prowl about the world seeking the ruin of souls."*

CHAPTER 6

'You're in Danger'

Amen. Amen to the Archangel Michael, who is not just important to Catholics but also to Jews and Muslims, to Protestants and non-denominationalists, to the Eastern Orthodox and even many Orientals.

Michael! He is the chief captain of the angels, the greatest warrior, the one who cast Satan out of Heaven in *Revelation* (12:7).

What a powerhouse. My heart lifts at the mention of his majestic name. He is the greatest of the angels, the greatest at any rate that we know of, not really just an "archangel" but of a power associated with the highest angelic orders. An angel more powerful than the potent fallen spirit called Lucifer.

To borrow from *A Dictionary of Angels* (by Gustav Davidson), Michael ranks as "the greatest of the angels whether in Jewish, Christian, or Islamic writings, secular or religious. He is chief of the order of virtues, chief of archangels, prince of the presence, angel of repentance, righteousness, mercy, and sanctification; also ruler of the fourth Heaven."

In 404 at the famous cave of the Archangel Michael on Monte San Angelo, in Italy, a wealthy man, frustrated when one of his cattle refused to move from the entrance of the cave, took up his bow and sent an arrow toward the animal. The arrow whirled about like a boomerang and came back to wound the archer. So frightened was this man that he went to see the bishop of Siponto, who decided there must be a mystery attached to the cave. He prayed that God's Will be revealed and thereupon a heavenly entity appeared to the bishop, saying, *"I am Michael the Archangel, who ever stands before the Lord. I am keeping this place under my special protection. By this strange occurrence, I wish to remind men to celebrate the Divine service in my honor and that of all the angels."*

Later, when Neapolitans decided to make war on Siponto, the bishop again sought heavenly direction and Michael appeared to him telling the bishop that the inhabitants should courageously meet the enemy and that despite the odds they would gain victory.

As soon as the attack began all of Monte Gargano, the highlands where the cave is located, was enveloped by a dark cloud which shot forth lightning of such strength as to chase away the enemy.

That is at any rate what is told to us through legend. We are told the great archangel also came to the assistance of Constantine the Great, helping him gain victory over the pagan emperor Maxentius.

In the 15th century when it seemed the Turks would conquer all of Europe, Michael again championed the cause of Christianity and led to a glorious victory over the infidels.

Saint Joan of Arc, who saved France, ascribed her victories to Michael.

Michael! He is the angelic prince of Israel, guardian of Jacob, known in Islamic writing as Mika'il. Some say he's the author of *Psalm* 85. In Jewish lore it's even believed that the fire Moses saw in the burning bush had Michael's appearance.

Christians invoke him as the angel of deliverance.

"Who is like unto God?" was Michael's war cry against the prideful fallen angels.

Along with Gabriel, Michael is the most commonly pictured angel in classic art, depicted often with wings and unsheathed sword. He is the warrior of God and holds the scales of justice.

In the recently discovered Dead Sea scrolls is a section entitled *War of the Sons of Light Against the Sons of Darkness.* Here Michael, according to one scholar, is referred to as "Prince of Light." He leads the angels of light against those of darkness. He's the patron of policemen. Besides *Revelation,* he also appears wrestling with Satan over the body of Moses in the testimony of Jude. He is the commander of nations (*Daniel* 12:1), and in the apocryphal Book of *Enoch* (9:1) he and the other archangels, looking down upon earth at the sorceries and lust of blood caused by demons, call upon the Lord to cleanse the world, which was when God replied that He would send the Flood.

I'll never know, not while I'm on earth, whether Michael was the entity symbolized in my dream, but I could often *feel* his presence. I could also feel the tension with demons. They tried to dissuade me from prayer. They instilled worrisome thoughts. They raised doubts about my rediscovered faith. They sought to lead me back into my old ways and to discourage me at every turn.

Like angels, demons have rank and status. There are higher orders and lower orders. Some are huge principalities, others are like nettlesome little scorpions.

And they're all around. Now I could see that. Now, through prayer, my spiritual blinders were lifting. I couldn't believe how suddenly my eyes opened to an entirely different reality.

Especially I thought back to the year after graduation from Fordham. It was during that time, in my early twenties, eight years before my dream, that I had conducted research into what I thought was the exciting new field of ESP and parapsychology. At the time bookstores were filled with volumes on meditation, alpha-training, spoonbenders, astrologers, numerologists, Hindu mystics, and pyramid power.

Psychic phenomena were all the rage, and so I was very curious when, as a cub reporter in 1975, I heard about a school teacher who was the center of great controversy because he was demonstrating ESP in the classroom. The local fundamentalists were calling him a witch and wanted him away from their children. I decided to write a feature story about this man and went to see him along with a

friend of mine, Donald Kennedy, who worked as an assis-
tant professor at the local state university.

Kennedy and I had been absolutely stunned by what we
saw. The school teacher was a very mild-mannered person
in his twenties who casually explained that he wasn't a
witch but a "psychic." He had paranormal abilities. That's
what had gotten him in hot water, he explained. He had
put on demonstrations of clairvoyance for the students, and
when their parents heard about that, he was in big trouble.
Soon there were large, heated meetings at which this
psychic school teacher was denounced and all but burned
at the stake.

I had two initial reactions. First, disdain for the "closed-
minded" locals who would denounce a psychic as a
"witch." Primitive thinking! I didn't have much time for
Bible-thumpers.

My second reaction, of course, was that of intense curiosity. I was still skeptical that supernatural powers actually
existed, and I wanted to see if the school teacher could
really do something outside of physical laws.

The teacher claimed he had clairvoyant powers, and so
I set up a test. I decided to hide my college ring in his
house and see if he could find it through "powers of the
mind." To make sure he wasn't peaking while I hid the
object I had Kennedy take him a block down the street.
When I was done I signaled them back.

The school teacher entered the house, closed his eyes for
a moment, as if in meditation, and then went right for the
kitchen cupboard, where I had hidden the ring in a container of teabags. It had taken him 17 seconds to find it.

You can imagine my reaction. I had stumbled for words.
And in a few minutes I was to become more wordless still.
As it turned out, this man also had what parapsychologists
call "psychokinesis." He was able to cause a table and
sometimes other objects to tilt upward and virtually levitate
in a way that seemed to defy physical laws. So astonished
was I that soon I brought in hypnotists and magicians to
try and explain it. Later I also took this psychic to the
Smith Hall of Physics at Kent State University to be
observed by Dr. Wilbur Franklin, who was chairman of the

graduate division and a scientist respected across America for his expertise with liquid crystals and his research into psychokinesis.

No one could explain what the teacher did. The man seemed to have the power to read minds and affect objects psychokinetically. A ticking or rapping erupted in wood he touched, and there was a distinct cool breeze.

The local magicians were beside themselves. They asked him to find a sewing needle—a *needle*—they had hidden somewhere in a three-bedroom apartment, and he found it in about fifty seconds. It was hidden in a stick of butter in the refrigerator!

I was terrifically excited and on April 7, 1975, after observing this man on a dozen occasions, including with a handful of other journalists, Kennedy and I wrote about the enigma for the local newspaper.

In Albany, Jack Maloy, state editor for United Press International, picked up the odd story and moved it across the newswire.

Thinking back, I didn't see any "evil" in that. The teacher certainly didn't seem sinister. After all, besides finishing up his school credits, he was a lay minister in the local Episcopal church. According to the scientists I had interviewed, including the famous J. B. Rhine of Duke, who coined the very term "extrasensory perception," psychics were simply in touch with an "energy" that science had not yet defined. It was mental phenomena, they assured me, not anything spiritual.

But thinking back about it years later, after my conversion, there were a few things that now disturbed me. When the teacher was doing his psychokinesis or whatever it was, a cool, inexplicable breeze had erupted in the room— a cold spot which parapsychologists called "clairsentience." They told me it had to do with energy dynamics, but it turned my neck to gooseflesh and ran chills up my spine.

When the teacher sat "levitating" tables, those strange rapping noises issued from the wood. Tap, tick, tap. He said they formed a code and he could communicate with them.

That smacked of "spirits." Had it been psychokinesis or

spiritualism? On occasion, this "psychic" would hold
hands with people in a circle, fall into a trance, and a spirit
voice would come through him.

What it was, really, was an old-fashioned seance.

I never did sit through one of his seances. The "spirit"
wouldn't come if I was in the house. He would wait until
I left. I had to rely on the testimony of other journalists
who came to witness it.

The spirit didn't seem to like me, and when I left behind
a tape recorder, trying to get his voice on a cassette, the
recorder would jam as soon as the spirit's brusque, tough
voice erupted from the usually mild-mannered school
teacher.

Finally I had set up *two* recorders before leaving the
house and both clicked off simultaneously and inexplicably when this "spirit" took over the teacher's body.

Sitting now two hundred miles away and eight years
later, in the midst of a tumultuous conversion in 1983, in
the wake of my dream, I began wondering if all that
phenomena, all that stuff that had intrigued me so when
I was 22 or 23, was more than it had seemed. Convinced
by the teacher that there might indeed be a spiritual realm,
I had also investigated a few homes that were supposedly
plagued by ghosts and had interviewed others who claimed
mental powers during the 1970s. This was why, years later,
I found the Chelsea townhouse so interesting. In a couple
cases I had even stayed overnight, listening for strange
sounds or other signs of supernaturality. It was back in the
mid-1970s. I was young and naive. I was searching. So
poor was my faith that I sought evidence of an afterlife,
evidence of a spirit world, in haunted houses instead of
in Christianity.

I remembered one house where it sounded like an old
woman was cackling in the middle of the night, and
another time when Kennedy and I rushed to an active
haunting and saw an incredible configuration of blue-white
light on the wall of a "haunted" bedroom.

We had watched that light for more than half an hour,
blocking the windows to make sure it wasn't an odd
reflection.

Like the levitating table, there was a coolness around it.

In Lewiston, New York, I investigated an old stone building known as the Frontier House that dated back to 1824 and had been a meeting place for a Masonic lodge. The likes of Charles Dickens, DeWitt Clinton, and Daniel Webster had slept there when it was an inn. Legend was that the Masons had abducted and murdered a man named William Morgan in 1826 when Morgan threatened to reveal their secrets. It was said the Frontier House was haunted by the ghost of Morgan.

Hmmm. That was very interesting to a 23-year-old journalist doing research in psychic phenomena. I went there and heard all kinds of stories from those who worked there. It had been converted into a restaurant that kept mysteriously burning down. One cleaning woman claimed to have seen an apparition, and Christmas deocrations were known to inexplicably disappear.

I went there a couple nights with a group of people listening as a strange clanking came from the basement, a metal gate that was opening and closing in the cellar.

It was exciting. It was scary. It was thrilling. But nothing evil. They were just spirits of the dead, right? More and more journalists were checking it out. Psychic stuff was news in the 1970s. There were even television documentaries about ghosts, including one hosted by Walter Cronkite.

Ghosts were harmless. Some psychics even encouraged people to speak with them.

It was a kick to visit a place and listen for eerie footsteps.

If the devil or Satan existed, I had decided, he was just a freak spirit who roamed the planet and occasionally bothered somebody like Linda Blair. That's how naive I was.

I'd had no idea about demons. I thought of things in terms of positive and negative "energies." To me it was a matter for science—not religion.

But as I reflected on my bygone years, as I looked back to 1975, I could see that even then God was trying to wake me up. I recalled the strange "coincidences" that had begun to occur when I was doing the research into psychic phenomena. One day, I remembered, I had gone to a small country church in Hale Eddy, New York, to observe a young woman, Patricia Jeffers, who spoke in "tongues." I figured religious phenomena might be just another form of psychic phenomena and I wanted to investigate it.

We were at the church, Patricia and I, and she was speaking in tongues. This was 1975. Suddenly there was a knock on the door. Three people. Three young strangers. A little older than I was. Two men and a woman, wanting to come in. It was obvious right off the bat that they were what everyone my age was calling "Holy Rollers." And right away I was turned off: I thought born-againers were old-fashioned and intellectually deficient.

The odd thing was that these three people said they were from New York City—which is more than a three-hour drive from Hale Eddy. They said they had awakened that morning and simply decided to drive wherever their hearts led them.

Which turned out to be the little non-denominational church where I was with the Jeffers woman.

"When we saw this church we just had to stop," said one of the men. Then he turned, stared for a moment, and pointed to me. "We're here because of you," he said suddenly. "You're in danger."

CHAPTER 7

Alone With God

*"Oh, God, in Jesus' name, we ask you again
to detach us from any occult contacts we've all
had in one form or another, sometimes without
knowing it, in this age where the occult has
infiltrated everywhere. Wash away the times we
harbored superstition, or read the astrology
column, or as youth played with pendulums or
palm reading, especially if we fooled with a
Ouija board. Or whatever, Lord. Cleanse us of
any spirit contact we may have had, wittingly or
unwittingly."*

Slowly, it was all coming back to me. Slowly, I began
to see the true spiritual realities.

"You're in danger."

Again I thought about those "Holy Rollers" and about
how I had been too smart, too worldly, too sophisticated
to heed them.

How had they known?

Who had sent them?

Why *hadn't* I listened back in 1975?

I was too smart. I wanted facts, ma'am, not religion. I
recalled the conversations I had with another born-again
Christian, Barbara Larnerd, who tried to convince me that

mysticism should be handled within the Church—not in physics laboratories. She later chronicled her arguments in a book called *Letters to Michael* (published by Christian Literature Crusade in 1977).

Her arguments fell on deaf ears. If I was going to involve myself with the supernatural, it was going to be *scientific.*

For a while psychic phenomena remained a side interest of mine. I realize now what I was being prepared for. But back then I was simply blind. I visited laboratories in Princeton and Brooklyn that were using the random-event generators to see if people could affect or predict the workings of a machine. I figured all the statistical evidence would convince atheists that there was indeed something more than flesh and blood—something more than the material world.

It had certainly convinced me. Although I soon went on to other things (except for occasionally listening to accounts such as that of the Chelsea townhouse), I knew what I had seen with the school teacher and what I experienced in haunted houses was paraphysical—beyond normal cause and effect.

I also figured that this undiscovered psychic energy could be used to heal people. I interviewed researchers who claimed a psychic named Dean Kraft had exploded HeLa cancer cells in a test tube, and in Buffalo I spoke with a Franciscan nun, Sister Justa Smith, who worked as a biochemist for Roswell Park Memorial Institute and had done experiments showing that a Hungarian "healer" named Oskar Estebany could speed up the activity of enzymes in a pyrex flask.

In January of 1974, two investigators named Philip B. Reinhart, a physicist, and Robert N. Miller, a chemical engineer, had also found that internationally-known healer Olga Worrall could affect a nuclear cloud chamber 600 miles away.

It certainly didn't seem like anything "occult" to me. As was the case with Dr. Owen, other prominent parapsychologists assured me that it wasn't the work of spirits but of psychoenergy. Many poltergeist cases involved girls who were at puberty, and the parapsychologists (they now call themselves "psi researchers") reasoned that puberty involves repressed emotions that occasionally express themselves in violent outbursts of psychic force—thus knocks in the wall and objects that move violently.

I questioned this. I questioned it because of the many cases where people saw apparitions, or heard voices, or communicated with the rapping noises. That didn't seem like psychokinesis. I questioned the cases that seemed like demonic possession.

But the parapsychologists drew the line at angels and demons. They didn't believe in them. ESP and mental power were okay, but demons were superstition.

Alone in my apartment, alone with God, invoking the Holy Spirit, I thought about those days of psychic research, and about the townhouse. There was something very wrong with that. It wasn't "psychokinesis." There was a malevolent spirit. Or *spirits.* I began to wonder about certain other peculiarities associated with Chelsea, such as the druggy women with leotards and heavy makeup who strode the streets, junk jewelry dangling, looking like they were in search of an Andy Warhol party or a Fellini movie. There was also a hotel where the punker Sid Vicious killed his seemingly possessed girlfriend.

Chelsea isn't far from Greenwich Village, which, albeit of higher quality, also had the same bizarre tastes. I remember walking through the village one night to see my agent and passing a middle-aged woman who was totally dressed in black with a strange hat and wearing the devil's symbol, a large metal pentagram. She looked like she was ready for Halloween.

Only in New York did witches advertise themselves right out on the streets.

Only in New York, and out in San Francisco, was witchcraft allowed to openly display itself.

One store in New York sold candles, ritual incense, belladonna, even old skulls which they implied (I never investigated further) were real.

On the extreme west side of Greenwich Village was a decadent homosexual community of sado-masochistic bars and sex clubs with names like "Hellfire."

CHAPTER 8

Rulers of Darkness

Was the phenomena in the townhouse just the tip of the iceberg?

Was evil something that, in a metaphysical sense, also afflicted society at large?

And if so was the evil in New York a condensation and harbinger of what was afflicting the rest of modern society?

It was like a curtain ringing up. Suddenly I saw before me an entirely different reality. Was it a "coincidence" that street bums and criminals often heard "voices"? Was it a matter of chance that many of those who were into drugs or homosexuality were also into the occult? Was it mere irony that they exhibited an actual revulsion to anything holy, especially anything to do with the Blessed Virgin Mary or Jesus?

In a discourse on August 13, 1986, Pope John Paul II quoted the Apostle John to the effect that "the whole world lies under the power of the evil one" (*1 John* 5:19). "The influence of the evil spirit can conceal itself in a more profound and effective way," added the Pope in his own words. "It is in his interest to make himself 'unknown.' Satan has the skill in the world to induce people to deny his existence in the name of rationalism and of every other system of thought which seeks all possible means to avoid recognizing his activity."

44

Upon visiting the famous shrine to the Archangel Michael at Monte Gargano in 1987, the Pope emphasized that "the disorder that lives in society, the incoherence of man, the interior breakdown of which mankind is victim, is not only the result of original sin, but also the effects of the dark and nefarious actions of Satan..."

As C. S. Lewis, the famous Anglican writer, reminded us (quoting I think from the poet Charles Baudelaire), the devil's cleverest wile is to convince us that he does not exist.

Suddenly I knew that what is in the New Testament is literally true. Our lives are made difficult, a never-ending struggle, by oppressive forces. "For we do not wrestle against flesh and blood, but against principalities, against powers, against the rulers of the darkness of this age, against spiritual hosts of wickedness in the heavenly places," says the Apostle Paul to the *Ephesians* (6:12).

How true. How awesome. Paul wasn't speaking about earthly powers and principalities but about the reality of demonic forces. And by virtue of my new sensitivity, which came in large part because of my brushes with actual powers of the dark, I was able now to rather readily feel or actually spot their presence. At times I actually envisioned their gruesome faces.

And to my shock I now saw how pervasive these forces are. I saw that they aren't just some kind of rare occurrence like those portrayed in horror movies. They're everywhere, and they are at constant work trying to influence us, recruit us, or failing that, to trip us up. I saw them in the eyes of gangsters, I felt them in the offices of "humanistic" magazines, I brushed against them in restaurants and bars.

I felt dirt, a brown spiritual dust, when I walked near Times Square and the shops overflowing with nearly unimaginably profane pornography.

When I passed a peep show or live-sex theatre I felt the same revulsion I felt around the Texas gangster.

The words "filth" and "sleaze" took on a new meaning. Something sickening, something antagonistic to the spirit, hovered around the smut shops, drug dealers, and prostitutes on 42nd Street.

It blared at you from boom boxes and flashed at you in a rush of lust from movies and television.

There was no more doubt in my mind: it is an actual energy. Evil is a force. It makes you tense. You feel sullied. You feel twinges of confusion and anxiety.

Yet at the same time there was great relief. Suddenly I knew that evil existed, but that also meant there was metaphysical good. God exists! He gives us more than enough weaponry to wade through the challenges. What a relief to see the real reason for so many disturbing things!

At times I didn't want to believe what I was seeing and feeling. I wanted to think I was delusional or over-reacting. Like the parapsychologists, I had thought belief in demonic entities was a sign of superstitiousness, religious fanaticism, or psychosocial imbalance.

But the sensations were too strong and consistent and I'm even more certain of that ten years later: negative spirits surround us. They are allowed to test us our whole lives, and their numbers are especially great in our particular era. As Paul told the Ephesians, we must "take up the whole armor of God, that you may be able to withstand in the evil day, and having done all, to stand. Stand therefore, having girded your waist with truth, having put on the breastplate of righteousness, and having shod your feet with the preparation of the gospel of peace; above all, taking the shield of faith with which you will be able to quench all the fiery darts of the wicked one.

"And take the helmet of salvation, and the sword of the Spirit, which is the word of God."

Alone in my apartment, I was starting to read the Bible every day. It dispelled evil with the same cleansing sensation as Holy Water. For the next few years after the dream, I couldn't get enough of Scripture. I read the King James version. I read the New American Bible. I read the *Reader's Digest* version. Sometimes I read all of *Psalms* in a single sitting.

It is a most powerful prayer, the *Psalms,* a miraculous praise of the Lord, and the more I prayed, the more I saw that what the Pope and C. S. Lewis said is only too true: evil is not just something we see in the eyes of a gangster, or around a woman practicing the occult, but comes in many varieties and forms. It's not just in the blatant manifestations, the revulsion one feels in passing a smut shop, but also insinuates itself into "respectable" aspects of society. I must admit that when I visited editors at many of the newspapers and magazines, I now felt the darkness and oppression of rationalism run amuck.

I also lost most of my friends. The two who worked in the newspaper business became upset when they heard I was going back to church; it was the last time I saw them. When another associate of mine in the publishing community, an important person in promoting my work, heard I was attending Mass, she actually shouted at me, "How can anyone with your intelligence go to *church!*" Shortly afterward, I dismissed her otherwise capable services.

Others sensed something without my mentioning anything about my rediscovered Christianity. On a subconscious level they could tell I was no longer one of them, especially those folks I knew in the secular media. Our spirits clashed and my work, once so quickly embraced, seemed now to bounce off of them. Soon those who had so ardently supported me downplayed my previous work and tried to undercut me. My entire idea of success was beginning to change. Once I had thought success meant success in the media. Now I believed success was contained in but one book, the Bible.

Imagine, a secular journalist turning into a "Holy Roller." Imagine, as a newborn Christian, an author whose work had been endorsed by the likes of Jane Fonda and who, on one research trip out west, used the office of her then husband Tom Hayden!

Me, a Christian, a man who occasionally wrote stories for no-nonsense publications like *Discover,* who had served for a short while as a contributing editor to *Science Digest,* and was a judge one year for the American Book Awards. Me, a journalist who had even written once for *Rolling Stone,* the avant-garde magazine!

I had no intentions of leaving that world, but suddenly we seemed to repel each other. There are many good people in the media, but there are also many who are antagonistic to Christ and badly misguided. For years after I returned to the Church I still functioned as a freelance journalist, but it wasn't the same. Nor was life in New York. I had loved New York. When I first moved to Manhattan I had embraced it, and it had embraced me. I liked the pace, the excitement, the intensity of information. I loved the food; it has the finest restaurants in the world. I liked the nightlife and glamor. Back in the 1980s, New York was happening. Until the stock market crashed, it was the hottest city going, and I lived in a good neighborhood. There wasn't much crime, and I was elbow to elbow with the world's movers and shakers. The richest man in the world, Daniel Ludwig, lived in the vicinity, as did Walter Cronkite, Gloria Vanderbilt, and Robert Redford. At the one neighborhood place, Elaine's, you could run into anyone from Woody Allen to Hollywood celebrities like Paul Newman and Cher.

I lived about a block from Elaine's, and while I was a pauper compared to many of those on the Upper East Side, I had enough cash in my jeans to have a good time. So lucrative was the college lecture circuit that I could do one or two talks and live off that for the next month and a half. Friends from Wall Street would take me to restaurants like Spark's or the Waterclub where a small group of us would blow close to a thousand bucks for dinner and wine.

It was an epic era. An epic era for Wall Street. An epic era for expense accounts. An absolutely epic era for greed. One fellow I knew paid himself a salary of $1 million a year from an oil brokerage business he owned, and that was before taking profits. Others on Park or Fifth avenues made even more than that, with weekend homes in Connecticut but summer homes on the French Riviera.

Yet it was all beginning to lose its lure. I began to pray hours a day, and as I did, it became tougher and tougher for me to deal with agnostic editors, or with friends who were atheists, using God's name only in vain, or with those whose sole interest was money. There's nothing wrong with making good money as long as it doesn't become an idol, and in Manhattan money was idol supreme. I was starting to get a bit turned off to New York, and New York was getting tired of me.

CHAPTER 9

'Behold, your mother'

On Good Friday of 1984, half a year after my dream, the most intense spiritual experience of my life occurred. This was no dream. It was sometime between noon and three, and I was praying non-stop to commemorate Our Lord's crucifixion.

Suddenly an image came tumbling into my mind's eye. It was an oval-shaped image, nearly like a large medal, but alive and rather three-dimensional, in color, different at any rate than any mental image I'd ever encountered.

It was the image of a holy and sweet woman whom I took to be Saint Mary, the Blessed Virgin.

There were no words, just the incredible still image. I saw her as an older woman, perhaps as Mary was a year or two before her death, with great humbleness, poverty and dignity. The image was so clear and penetrating, so full of motherly love, that it went right to my soul. She was beautiful, but not in the physical sense. She was beautiful in *spirit*.

Later, when I first heard of Medjugorje (where the Blessed Mother was appearing to six children), I was skeptical because the visionaries there described a *young* woman—indeed, a woman of 19 or 20—while the Virgin I "saw" was old. The face was very similar to a miraculous icon known as the Virgin of Seven Sorrows, a reproduction of which I later purchased in Cuencha, Ecuador.

In a way that I can't explain, this simple and wordless encounter had a tremendously profound effect on me. It greatly heightened my devotion to the Virgin. It greatly piqued my interest in her other manifestations. For me it was a watershed event. I picked up booklets that had to do with the apparitional sites of Lourdes and Guadalupe and Fatima.

Although I have listened with interest for years to many objections about the role of Mary, I could never forget the graces I've received and continue to receive through her real and maternal intercession. She is a messenger, a fore-runner, a mother, given a special role by Our Lord. She is specially honored in Heaven because of her suffering and faith on earth. The agony of a mother watching her son die so horribly, beaten and nailed to wood, is beyond my imagination, and perhaps this was why I saw her on Good Friday: That was the day Jesus, in one of His last instructions to an apostle, told John, and thus told us all, *"Behold, your mother"* (*John* 19:27).

Like everything Christ uttered, it was meant to be heard not just by John but by everyone down through the generations.

"Behold, your mother."

It cannot be stressed enough that she is an intercessor and does not usurp the authority of her Son, who has sent her; instead she constantly points to Christ and prepares His way, as she did 2,000 years ago. Why is she not mentioned more in the Bible? Perhaps it's because she had so humbled herself. It certainly isn't because she didn't have a crucial role to play. Indeed, significant parts of the New Testament are based on what could only have been *her* recollections (see the very first chapter of *Matthew,* to start with), and that's why she's probably not mentioned too much: she was humble and didn't thrust herself in a position of prominence. She simply served the Will of God, bore Jesus and, with Joseph, reared the Messiah.

As for her role and the effectiveness of asking her help, we have only to read another part of the New Testament, *John* 2:1-10, in which Mary successfully nudges Jesus into causing His first public miracle (the turning of water into wine) despite His initial reluctance.

That's exactly what she does now: tries to get us a little leeway and some extra graces, even when we don't fully deserve them.

We ask people here on earth to pray for us, so why not ask saints like Mary, who are in Heaven and thus closer to God?

Mary is an *advocate*. She goes to her Son with our requests. She puts in an extra word for us. She tells us (at places like Medjugorje) that we should go directly to Christ, who is the only mediator between God and man, but it certainly doesn't hurt to get an extra boost from His earthly mother.

This is not praying *to* Mary. This is not making her a goddess. It's asking for her potent prayers *("Holy Mary, mother of God, pray for us sinners...")*. Surely Christ is pleased when His mother is honored, as anyone is happy when one's mother is honored, and her manifestations go back to the first century, 1,400 years before there was a parting of the ways between Catholics and Protestants.

Even Martin Luther recognized the influence Mary swayed with Jesus and carried on a devotion to her until he was about 40. Walking through the countryside in 1503, he accidentally cut his leg with his sword, a deep gash that endangered his life. "Oh Mary, help me!" Luther cried. Though he later began backing away, for years he had a picture of her in his room. "We do not want to make an idol out of Mary, but to celebrate for God's honor," he said. "I saw that Mary does not desire to be an idol; she does nothing; God does all. We ought to call upon her that for her sake God may grant and do what we request. Thus also, all other saints are to be invoked, so that their work may be every way God's alone."

The Virgin, added Luther, "is in the middle between Christ and all other men."

That she should now come in apparition is no different than two other biblical figures, Moses and Elijah, appearing in apparition to the apostles Peter, James and John (*Matthew* 17:1-3). In fact, communication directly from

Heaven in the form of apparition or locution is at the foundation of both Judaism and Christianity—from Adam and Noah (see *Genesis*) to the experiences of Abraham by the terebinth trees of Mamre.

Throughout the Bible angels materialize and speak to mankind, the most noteworthy being the apparition of an angel (*Luke* 1:26-35) to Mary herself.

Of course, the most famous corporeal apparitions were those of Christ Himself after His crucifixion.

Need I really mention all that? We must function in the Spirit, and in the Spirit I could feel demonic attacks cease as I prayed the Rosary, replaced by a tremendously pleasant flow of joy and peace. The Virgin's image had gone straight into my heart, bearing only good fruits, leading me on the path toward Jesus. She is my buddy. She's a prayer-warrior. She's my heavenly mother, and boy did I need her. I was still in the throes of deliverance, and I was still struggling in the cold hard world of journalism.

I remember rising early one morning to appear again on *The Today Show.* There are always tensions associated with national TV—you want things to go right, in the few available moments—and the situation was compounded by the fact that I was to appear with the New Jersey gangster, who was incognito at a satellite studio in Atlanta.

I was also a bit concerned about hailing a taxi so early in the morning, for as I recall we were to be in studio at Rockefeller Center by 6:30 a.m.

Taking time out for prayer, I stood in my living room, saying a Rosary. I prayed from the heart, and with confidence. I even prayed for the taxi. There was great grace flowing, and just as I finished the very last bead, the sun rose over the horizon and suddenly split through my blinds in the form of a perfect cross.

For a minute or two, there was this large and perfectly formed cross coming through my blinds with incredible radiance.

The interview, conducted by Bryant Gumble, went exceedingly well, but what I remember most is that on leaving my apartment there was a taxi sitting right there at the corner of 90th Street, as if waiting for me.

CHAPTER 10

Creatures of the Night

I felt bold in the Lord. I felt confident. When a jewel thief from Miami threatened me because I'd put his name in my book, I didn't give it much thought. I just prayed about it—and never heard from him again. When I was under a tight deadline for an article, or under pressure on the college lecture circuit, all I needed was to take the time for some Scripture or the Rosary.

The beautiful feelings flowed. The peace and grace. I prayed for hours at a time, and the tranquility gave me the greatest joy of my life. I felt an actual glow.

Yet there were still things to sort through.

I could deal with the Mafia stuff. I could handle environmental controversies. But I still had one major fear. I still feared demonic attacks and the invisible entity—that despicable hounding enemy, that unrelenting spirit—called Satan.

I was afraid because the more I prayed and read Scripture, the more Lucifer attacked. The demons continued their rage. The closer I got to God, the more numerous were their fiery darts.

One morning, visiting my parents, I woke only to see, with eyes wide open, what I believe to this day to have been a tall demonic presence, terribly dark and helmeted, next to the couch. It vanished after a split second, but for weeks after I was terrified.

It was not a dream, nor was it in any way hallucinatory. It scared me to the bottom of my soul. Like my three-part dream, it imprinted itself indelibly on my memory. I didn't see any facial features. He was too dark. He was blacker than a shadow. I didn't see the face but I could sense this overwhelming anger. He was there to intimidate me.

Had I listened to my dream I would have simply raised my hand and said "Vanish!"

But I'd been too cowardly to do anything.

I didn't realize a few central truths. First, that evil spirits have a bark that's worse than their bite. Oh, they do have somewhat of a bite, but they're like dogs on a leash and can truly hurt you only if you place yourself within their range. The second important truth is that the worst thing we can *do* is fear them. Fear of the devil gives him power and energy. Fear of the devil is faith in the devil's power. Faith unlocks what power the devil has—when we should be showing faith in Him who is infinitely more powerful.

I once asked a mystic how powerful Satan is in relation to God. If the Lord is the Empire State Building, I wanted to know, how tall is Satan? I figured at least a two or three-story building.

This particular mystic, who'd been shown visions of demons and Hell, looked at me with a bemused smile and said, "Let me get this straight. You want to know, if God is the Empire State Building, how big is the devil next to Him?"

I nodded.

"If God is the Empire State Building," said this wise mystic, "then Satan is smaller than a grain of sand."

Of course to us he seems gigantic, and if we don't have faith, he *is*. Satan is also huge in the lives of those who know nothing about him. It behooves us spiritually to know and confront him in the Holy Spirit. With the great forces of the Spirit! But we have to tread with caution. After all, this is a superhuman entity who once ranked high among angels. He's far smarter than we are.

But we only make it worse when we fear. I now find discussing demons, in the correct perspective, to be a cleansing experience. We must be careful not to be curious or obsessed—not to give demons more than their due—but we must also bring them into the light, which they hate. To do so is to bring ourselves spiritual joy, for identifying the mechanism of a disease is a step toward rejoicing in the vigors of health. "Likewise," says one demonologist, Father Randall Paine, "discovering that there is an infernal method in the madness of the world can be comforting light to souls teased with absurdities and tempted by despair. It actually relieves the mind to discover a reason for the wrongness of things, even if the reason is rather creepy."

The great Anglican writer G. K. Chesterton added: "The Christian way is to believe there is a positive evil somewhere and fight it; for then everything else will be really jolly and pleasant...Roses will be twice as red if you believe in the devil. Skies will be twice as blue..."

That's the joy of spiritual awareness, and besides, you have to know the enemy to win a war. What do demons look like? Anything they want to look like. Often we "see" them in our subconscious, which, like the imagination, is a form of perceiving device. Without knowing it many Hollywood writers have come very close to portraying them in their movies. Take a look at the creatures in *Star Wars,* or Freddie Krueger, or *Gremlins.* That's what demons look like, disfigured humans or otherworldly creatures—entities that seem half human, half animal. And all evil. They range in manifestation from immaterial fleas and scorpions, from spiritual bats, to gruesome ewoks and ETs.

The more powerful ones might put us in mind of Darth Vader. Like the angelic realm, there are various levels of demons. There are former angels, archangels, principalities, powers, dominations, thrones, cherubim, and seraphim. They are anti-angels.

Ten years ago, if someone had said what I just said to you, I would have told them to take three Excedrin and see Woody Allen's psychotherapist. At the very least I would have searched their shirt pockets for funny cigarettes. *Demons!* Give me a break. Last time they were big was back when people burned witches up in Salem.

Demons: but now I know they exist, and that, as the Bible says, there are different manifestations of them. They come in many shapes and forms. They are legion. There are millions of them. The New Testament is absolutely full of accounts whereby Jesus heals people by first casting out unclean spirits. In fact there are 51 passages in the Gospel relating to expulsion of demons. The first mention of the word "demon" is in *Deuteronomy,* and as for Jesus, *Matthew* (4:24) tell us that "they brought to Him all sick people who were afflicted with various diseases and torment, and those who were demon-possessed, epileptics, and paralytics; and He healed them."

In *Matthew* 9:33, we are told about a mute man who was healed as soon as he was delivered from the spirit possessing him.

The effect of demons seemed to also occur in epilepsy and diseases of the nervous system. A paralytic was healed when Jesus forgave him his sins.

So too were demons present in what we now call mental or psychological afflictions. What better example of this than when Christ (*Mark* 5:1-9) encounters a demented man who wears no clothes and lives in the tombs, a fiercely wild man whom they could not constrain. "And always, night and day, he was in the mountains and in the tombs, crying out and cutting himself with stones," said Mark.

Jesus demanded the unclean spirit to leave this poor man, and when he asked the demon its name, it replied, "My name is Legion; for we are many."

Once they were cast out and sent into a herd of swine the demented man regained his wits and was normal again—clothed, calm, and clean in body and mind.

Think of the old term for insanity: *dementia.*

Somehow we forgot all that. Somehow demons are no longer believed and no longer preached. There is tremendous resistance to discussing spirits of darkness, yet they play a heavy part in our every day, and they are especially prevalent around those who sin. To deliver the famous prostitute, Mary Magdalen, Christ had to cast out (*Mark* 16:9) seven demons.

But they also afflict those who have taken the path

toward God. It's part of the challenge of living. "A difficult struggle against the powers of darkness pervades the whole history of man," concluded the Second Vatican Council. "The battle was joined from the very origins of the world and will continue until the last day, as the Lord has attested." Victims of demonic attack have included Saint Catherine of Siena, Saint Teresa of Avila, Padre Pio, Saint Francis of Assisi, Saint John Bosco, and Saint Rose of Lima.

But they didn't fear because they kept in mind that God has limited the devil's power.

"If the devil could do everything he wanted, there would not remain a single living human being on the earth," said Saint Augustine.

While the existence of wicked angels requires that we remain ever watchful so as not to yield to their empty promises, we can be certain that the victorious power of Christ overcomes them at every turn if we have faith. He is the Redeemer.

"There is no need to be afraid to call the first agent of evil by his name: the Evil One," said Pope John Paul II in an apostolic letter aimed at the youth. "The strategy which he used and continues to use is that of not revealing himself, so that the evil implanted by him from the beginning may receive its development from man himself, from systems and from relationships between individuals, from classes and nations—so as also to become ever more a 'structural' sin, ever less identifiable as 'personal' sin. In other words, so that man may feel in a certain sense 'freed' from sin but at the same time ever more immersed in it."

Most of my life I had been oblivious to evil spirits. Most of my life I had ascribed anxiety or troubles or misfortunes as just that—bad luck, quirks of a new science called psychology. I had never heard anything about demons at Mass or church school, and certainly not at Fordham University, where one Jesuit professor I knew, now a prominent editor at a liberal Catholic newspaper, scoffed at the notion of devils and Satan.

That is what the Evil One wants: cynics and scoffers. I was no longer a scoffer. After my dream, after my own brush with a demonic force, after seeing with my own eyes, I realized that the New Testament is not just a book of morals but a complete guide to life that has to be taken literally. If demons were so commonplace in Jesus' time, the same must be true today. And it is. I began perceiving that simple truth all around me. At times, when I saw an addict or a wino, I felt a little of the same spiritual grit I'd felt around the gangsters.

Were demons infesting some of those poor homeless folks, the ones who were filthy and sleeping on the sidewalk grates?

Were they like the man in the country of the Gadarenes who lived in the tombs and was possessed by a "legion" of unclean spirits?

I remember a homeless person on the corner of 89th Street and Third Avenue who tried to attack me one afternoon in 1986 as he stood scrounging from a trash container. It was entirely unprovoked. I hadn't so much as glanced at him. He waved a long stick and had a fierce glint in his eyes.

To one degree or another, evil spirits plague us all. They cause anger—sudden shifts in mood. They cause coolness and arrogance. They cause confusion and negativity.

When we sin, or when we entertain thoughts offered us by such spirits, we open the door and let them in. They hover around us, plaguing us from the outside with doubts and misfortune or infiltrating our very bodies as in the case of Mary Magdalen.

They're allowed increasing dominance the longer we wallow in pride, lust, anger, faithlessness, or jealousy. They open the door through drugs and alcohol. They find an open door through greed and materialism and especially sexual immorality.

And they *hate* holiness. They hate the Word of God, which *Ephesians* tells us is the sword against demonic entities. They hate the aura of Jesus. I'll never forget another time, walking down Third Avenue after an especially long session of uplifting prayer. I felt surrounded by grace. I'd been praying for I don't know how long, and I went to run an errand.

It was rush hour, and the folks who worked in areas like Wall Street were coming from the 86th Street subway station. I spotted a bearded, well-dressed man. He looked like a lower-level stockbroker, and it was very strange. He was gritting his teeth and talking to himself. He was strutting up Third in the opposite direction and swinging his head back and forth. You could tell he was about to erupt in violence. He was actually growling, and he had that glaze across his eyes.

Suddenly between 87th and 88th this man caught sight of me and for no reason stepped from the onrushing throngs and lunged at me.

I ignored him and went about my business, but I knew I had just experienced something out of the ordinary. We had not really made eye contact as we passed each other, nor was I in his way. It was as if he sensed the prayerful aura and was going to attack it. Or I should say that the *thing* in him was going to attack me. The same happened in the cafes. I began to notice how some of the people, especially when they were well into their cups, took on new and insidious personalities. I saw looks in their eyes that left me with crawly skin. I recall one man, out of his mind on cocaine, who had taken a seat next to me and kept murmuring under his breath, in a voice deeper than his own, "I'll kill you. I'm going to kill you."

He was the brother of a famous singer who had a hit song at the time that mentioned a "creature of the night."

CHAPTER 11

Over Mean Streets

But whenever demons are around, so is the vastly more powerful force called the Holy Spirit. So are Christ and the angels. So is Mary.

I had any number of confrontations with evil spirits, too many to recount here, too ugly to *want* to recount, but I had just as many overwhelmingly pleasant experiences. Most of them were simple feelings. I was *happier.* I was less tense. I felt waves of grace as I prayed or read the New Testament.

There were little manifestations that seemed to be giving me clues or sending me messages. They were little treats. Most of the experiences, for whatever reason, came in dreams. Or in the sweetness of a heavenly coincidence. I began to realize that there really are no such things as "coincidences." Oh, a few here and there, but many of those we meet, many of the situations in which we find ourselves, are for hidden reasons.

Right after the little incident in which the crazed guy with the beard lunged at me on Third Avenue, I was walking up the east side of the avenue, it might even have been on the way home that same day, and when I got to the front of my apartment, moving in the river of pedestrians at rush hour, an old woman suddenly stood in front of me. She

was right in my path. I had to stop. I didn't see her coming.
She stood there facing me and, smiling a terrifically sweet
smile, she made the sign of the cross—as if blessing me.
I felt a beautiful wave of grace move through my being,
completely dispelling the antagonisms of the day.

This unusual woman said nothing, just smiled and then
disappeared into the sidewalk crowd.

She was about 70, and I think she might have been one
of the women from church, but I never was able to spot
her again.

I just know she made me feel that someone *was* watching
over me.

I don't like relating these personal experiences but feel
I must when they are pertinent and have meaning. I don't
want to relate them because I'm certainly no visionary and
because I know some of you will have difficulty with such
manifestations.

Besides, I am myself skeptical of many such claims.

I'm also aware that those of you who are Protestant are
by now concerned with the Catholic nature of my little
brushes with mysticism.

But it would be dishonest to ignore my own personal
observations. You discern their veracity. I'm simply report-
ing what I *believe* I saw, what I *believe* came from somewhere other than my subconscious.

One night I couldn't sleep, which was unusual for me.
I rarely have a problem falling off to slumber. I pray myself
to sleep.

But this one night I couldn't get there, and so finally I
gave up and went into the living room. It was about half
past midnight on a weeknight, I think a Wednesday. I was
sitting on my couch looking at the dark skyline of New
York when I noticed what seemed like a small pale blue
light, a globule of luminosity, amidst the apartment buildings between Third and Lexington.

At first I thought it was a distant television. Maybe it
was. It was unsteady light, flickering. There are so many
buildings and windows in Manhattan, who knows what it
might have been? I couldn't exactly place it. The light
seemed to be nearly a block down 90th, on the north side,

moving around that part of the neighborhood against the backdrop of six-story apartment buildings.

I struggled to define its origin. Was it first one television, then a television in another apartment, and was that what made it seem to move about? I couldn't tell. The important point is that as I looked into that flickering blue light I saw a frontal etching—just an outline—of the Virgin Mary.

This was no apparition. It wasn't even a vision. If anything it was a manifestation. It was nothing like what I had seen on Good Friday in 1984. It was vaguer, like a distinct etching, but there was no question it was a veiled head that resembled the Virgin. The chin, cheeks, and eyes were all very distinct, and so was the mouth.

I blinked and looked and it was still there. I looked away and looked back and still I saw her in an azure globule that continued flickering.

I walked to my kitchenette and probably got a glass of water, and when I looked back over the dark, mean streets, she was still in the small wavering light.

I did the logical thing: I lit a cigarette, took a puff, and convinced myself it was a television set. It seemed to move, first at one apartment building, then at another, and I decided it was because there were still folks up watching TV.

At night, when most other lights are out, you notice television sets flickering from the skyscrapers in New York. They take on excessive optical prominence because they are generating light from dark rooms. Staring at such a light can play tricks on the eyes and brain.

Whether or not that's what it was, it seemed to be moving around, first at a height of six stories, then at the level of, say, a third floor. In it, filling the luminous bubble, was the distinct womanly face. I watched it for at least 15 minutes. I was astonished. I felt blessed, full of grace. I even crushed out the cigarette.

But then another image took Mary's place. In the same light, as if shoving her away, I saw, to my surprise, the etched face of a malefic entity—the devil or one of his demons.

No way had I expected that. I looked away. I wasn't terrified, just very concerned. It was not nearly as upsetting as what I had seen in the dream, nor what I had seen that morning on the couch, but it was still alarming. I wondered if it indicated that the entire manifestation, including Mary's face, was a demonic counterfeit—if the whole thing wasn't an evil little charade.

I don't think so. I think it was a little clue as to spiritual warfare. At the time it didn't mean much, but as I look back it was showing me the nature of a raging battle, one that we're all called to join, on one side or another. Mary and the demon, vying for the place in the little flickering globe of light, the demon trying to crowd her out of view, even if it was just my imagination. I watched this little contention go on for another ten or fifteen minutes before going back to sleep.

How meaningful that little display would become when I began researching Saint Mary's apparitions. It was just a tiny example of manifestations erupting throughout the world during the 1980s. I didn't know it at the time, but the Blessed Virgin Mary had already been appearing for several years at Medjugorje in the Bosnia-Hercegovina republic of Yugoslavia. Medjugorje! She was appearing to peasant teenagers there, admonishing that peace was in a state of crisis (although at the time there was absolutely no indication that soon there would be a civil war) and dispensing warnings about the future of the world. She was also manifesting in Africa and Syria and Argentina.

I heard nothing about that; I knew nothing about Medjugorje. None of my friends were practicing Catholics, and I had never even heard of a "Marian movement." I had never heard of Knock or LaSalette. I didn't even know the full story of Lourdes and Fatima.

I was a loner. I had no connections. I went to church and came home.

How could I have known about Mary's appearances? They certainly weren't on *Nightline*. But appearing she was. Unbeknownst to me, it was claimed she was manifesting at a coptic church in East Brunswick, New Jersey (where Orthodox parishioners saw an image of her on a window and videotaped it) and on the west side of Chicago, where an icon of her actually wept.

Another icon was weeping in Greece, and a statue of the Virgin was shedding blood in the Philippines.

In Paris a man named Bassam Assaf claimed to be seeing Mary as an apparition, and hundreds more claimed to see the Virgin down in Betania, Venezuela.

I knew none of that. I knew only that I was a secular journalist having strange experiences—experiences I mentioned to no one—alone in my apartment at 200 East 90th Street.

Using my Scriptural Rosary, I often took the subway down to Saint Patrick's Cathedral and prayed in the small chapel at the back before a beautiful statue of Mary sculpted by Oronzio Maldrelli. On two or three visits I experienced something out of the ordinary in that chapel. Looking up, the statue's face seemed to twitch—mouth moving upward in a fuller smile. Perhaps it was an optical illusion. Perhaps my eyes were tired.

But I felt incredible in that chapel, and I felt a nearness to Mary that is beyond words. It was as if she was smiling down upon me.

I didn't know it, but at that very time statues were also coming to life in Ireland. In about 25 spots throughout that nation—which has close ties to Saint Patrick's—hundreds were claiming to see manifestations at roadside grottos. Statues were twitching there too, or even turning into full-blown apparitions. It started in Ballinspittle, which is south of Cork, and spread up through Mount Melleray as far north as Bessbrook.

I had not heard of that at the time, so it certainly wasn't a case of psychological suggestion. Rather it was another little manifestation in an outbreak that would soon reach epic proportions. Mary was in the world. So was the Archangel Michael. I didn't know it, but the very year I had my dream of Michael, but on the other side of the world, in the unreachable depths of Soviet Russia, Josyp Terelya, leader of the underground Catholic Church, also saw Michael in a vision. It was about three months before my experience, and I find it a "coincidence" that I later wrote Terelya's autobiography, *Witness,* for him.

At the time, Terelya, a Ukrainian mystic and Catholic activist, was in a Russian prison. On July 17, 1983, he

wrote his wife Olena that he had a vision in which he was
at the famous shrine of Zarvanystya south of Ternopil when
suddenly an intense light illuminated the vegetation.

A large white eagle came and settled on the field and
told him he should not fear.

In the distance Terelya saw an old man dressed in white.
The man introduced himself as the Archangel Michael and
predicted that great miracles would occur in several years,
miracles that would be witnessed by hundreds of thousands. This prophecy was later fulfilled when huge crowds
witnessed manifestations of Mary in 1987 and 1988 at the
shrine of Zarvanystya and at a chapel in Hrushiw, Ukraine.
It was also a true prophecy about Medjugorje, where not
thousands but *millions* would soon report spiritual
phenomena.

*"The Lord is now gathering the good men against the
evil,"* Michael told him. *"The world would long ago have
been destroyed but the soul of the world would not allow
this. As the soul preserves the life of the body, so do Christians preserve the life of the world. God needs fervent and
constant sons. You shall go through the ways of the world
and give witness, and in the end God will punish the
apostates because only through this punishment will God
be able to bring man back to sound reason. And when the
faith and love shall be reborn, Satan will begin a new
persecution of the Christians. Times of persecution will
begin, of priests and the faithful. The world will be divided
into the messengers of God and messengers of anti-christ.
After the great revelations of the Virgin Mary, renewal of
love of Christ will begin."*

CHAPTER 12

Hellfire

A battle loomed. It was to be a crucial contest in the invisible dimension around us, a battle in the lower depths and the heavenlies. This basic message, that supernatural war was upon us, had been the theme of apparitions not only at Hrushiw and Medjugorje, but since 1830 at Rue du Bac in Paris, the "Miraculous Medal" appearances, when Saint Mary announced the coming of a difficult age to the nun Catherine Labouré. *"The entire world will be overcome by evils of all kind,"* said our Blessed Mother. *"The moment will come when the danger will be great. All will seem lost. But have confidence!"*

A few years later, on September 19, 1846, Mary reappeared at the other side of France, on an alpine mountain above the hamlet of LaSalette, to two peasant children who were given longer and starker messages, including a warning that demons were soon to be loosed from Hell. She said to look out for performers of miracles, which made me think of psychics like the teacher who levitated tables, and she warned that spirits of the dead would appear *("brought back to life")* but in reality would be demons in disguise, which put me in mind of the Chelsea townhouse.

Not too long after LaSalette, Pope Leo XIII had a premonition of the coming evils. It's claimed that on October 13,

1884, having celebrated the Holy Sacrifice, the aged pontiff was in conference with the cardinals. Suddenly the Pope sank to the floor in a deep swoon. Doctors who rushed to his side feared that he had already expired, for, supposedly, they could find no trace of the Pope's pulse. However, after a short interval the Holy Father rallied, and opening his eyes, exclaimed with great emotion: 'Oh, what a horrible picture I was permitted to see!' He had been shown in spirit the tremendous activity of evil spirits. It was at this time he wrote the St. Michael prayer (page 32).

On December 26, 1957, Lucia dos Santos, a cloistered nun and the only surviving visionary from the famous apparitions in 1917 at Fatima, Portugal, had told an inquirer that the devil was "in the mood for engaging in a decisive battle against the Virgin. And a decisive battle is where one side will be victorious and the other side will suffer defeat."

Our Blessed Mother promised at Fatima that *"in the end my Immaculate Heart will triumph,"* leaving us no doubt about the final outcome. She told us there that **God** wished to establish devotion to her Immaculate Heart, and she greatly stressed prayer for sinners.

At Medjugorje, where Mary was working hardest at gathering her army, the visionary Mirjana Dragicevic allegedly was shown the devil during a 1982 apparition. "As usual I had locked myself into my room alone and was waiting for the Madonna," she said. "I knelt down...and suddenly there was a flash of light and Satan appeared...He was horrible...black all over...terrifying. I felt weak and fainted. When I came to, he was still standing there, laughing...He told me I would be very beautiful and very happy in love and life, and so on, but I would have no need of the Madonna or of my faith. 'She has brought you nothing but suffering and hardships,' the devil said. He, on the other hand, could give me everything I wanted."

When Mirjana rejected him, Mary arrived and the devil immediately disappeared. *"Excuse me for this, but you must realize that Satan exists,"* the Virgin Mary explained. *"One day he appeared before the throne of God and asked permission to submit the Church to a period of trial. God gave him permission to try the Church for one century. This century is under the power of the devil, but when the secrets confided to you come to pass, his power will be destroyed. Even now he is beginning to lose his power and has become aggressive. He is destroying marriages, creating division among priests and is responsible for obsessions and murder. You must protect yourselves against these things through fasting and prayer, especially community prayer. Carry blessed objects with you. Put them in your house and restore the use of holy water."*

Was the battle about to enter its final hour? The fires of Hell were *raging.* That was the reason, said Mary, that she was coming with the same force as she had at LaSalette and Fatima, indeed with even greater force, *"giving you messages as it has never been done in history since the beginning of the world."*

We had to find salvation, she said, *"while there is time."*

The present hour, Mary warned, *"is the hour of Satan. The hour has come when the demon is authorized to act with all his force and power."*

At Medjugorje the young visionaries claim they were shown a sea of fire and one of them, Marija Pavlovic, watched a pretty woman enter the flames and come out as a grotesque figure—half human, half beast, but different than any earthly animal.

This was very similar to a vision of Hell given in 1917 to the Fatima visionaries. Recalled Lucia: "Plunged in this fire were demons and souls in human form, like transparent burning embers, all blackened or burnished bronze, floating about in the conflagration, now raised into the air by the flames that issued from within themselves together with great clouds of smoke, now falling back on every side like sparks in a huge fire, without weight or equilibrium, and amid shrieks and groans of pain and despair, which horrified us and made us tremble with fear. The demons could be distinguished by their terrifying and repellent likeness to frightful and unknown animals, all black and transparent. This vision lasted but an instant. How can we ever be grateful enough to our kind heavenly Mother, who had already prepared us by promising in the first apparition to take us to Heaven. Otherwise, I think we would have died of fear and terror.''

Another time Lucia and her two cousins, Francisco and Jacinta Marto, were playing when Francisco withdrew to a hollow among the rocks.

"A considerable time had elapsed, when we heard him shouting and crying out to us and to Our Lady," recalled Lucia. "Distressed lest something might have happened to him, we ran in search of him, calling out his name. 'Where are you?' 'Here! Here!' But it still took us some time before we could locate him. At last, we came upon him, trembling with fright, still on his knees, and so upset that he was unable to rise to his feet. 'What's wrong? What happened to you?' In a voice half smothered with fright, he replied: 'It was one of those beasts that we saw in Hell. He was right here breathing out flames!' "

The hellfire was also seen by popes. They warned of coming decadence. They said humanity was in a state worse than at any time since the Flood. In the words of Pope Pius XII, there was a terrific struggle "which grows in proportion and in violence; so it is necessary for all Christians to be up and ready to fight to the death. We speak of the battle that evil, under its myriad forms, launches against good; the struggle of hate against love, of evil habits against purity, of egoism against social justice, of violence against the peaceful life, of tyranny against liberty."

He foresaw the decay of morals on all sides "fostered by evil shows, evil books, evil newspapers" and "the breakdown of the very foundations of society."

This was the era of "cosmic consciousness." This was the era of Shirley MacLaine. On the college circuit, speaking on toxic contamination, I noticed an alarming change: audiences were now composed largely of New Age types whose agenda was to establish a nature-goddess consciousness. No longer did they speak of ecology in terms of danger to humans. In Santa Clarita a convicted prostitute and self-anointed priestess of a sex-based religion would soon work three days a week taking children on hikes at a nature center.

In Oakland there was an institute run by Matthew Fox, a Dominican priest (now defrocked) whose staff included a practicing witch named Starhawk.

Back in New York, every December, musical archdruid Paul Winter, a New Age saxophonist and composer, was allowed to stage a "Winter Solstice Whole Earth Celebration" in the cavernous sanctuary of Saint John the Divine Episcopalian Cathedral. Another guest at the church was David Spangler, one of the world's pre-eminent New Agers and a man who believes that Lucifer is not a force of evil but comes to give us "wholeness." An advocate of Luciferic initiation was speaking during Eucharistic services! The cathedral also housed an ecumenical task force called the "Temple of Reason," which was directed, in part, by a Manhattan priest who associated with a mysterious occult organization called Lucis Trust—whose publishing branch was once called Lucifer Publishing.

At places such as Mankato State University in Minnesota, Catholic nuns as well as participants from the American Baptist, Disciples of Christ, United Church of Christ, United Methodist, and Presbyterian denominations attended "women and spirituality" conferences that included a *wiccan* ceremony on Sunday. *Wicca* is the religion of witchcraft!

This was all in accordance with the prophecies of LaSalette, where Mary warned that many convents would no longer serve as houses of God but would instead become *"the grazing grounds for Asmodeus* (in Jewish demonology an evil spirit)." All justice would be trampled underfoot and *"only homicides, hate, jealousy, lies, and dissension"* would be seen, said the LaSalette Madonna, correctly anticipating a crime rate that now includes 25,000 homicides or cases of non-negligent manslaughter a year. In one New York neighborhood, the 75th precinct in Brooklyn, a murder occurs on average every 63 hours!

Such was the fruit of a society that, as the Blessed Mother forecast, had gone *"cold and secular."* It was a result of demons rising from the hellfire as a test and punishment for all of mankind. They had already pervaded the mass media, especially nudie magazines such as *Playboy,* which twisted the minds and sensibilities of an entire generation.

Naturally the publisher of *Playboy,* Hugh Hefner, railed against the Church and openly promoted "sex without love," declaring, in his eerie editorials, that the Ten Commandments were out of date.

That was the "soft-core" pornography. The X-rated or "hardcore" stuff went beyond the explicit into the realm of nausea. In Times Square, right there in storefront windows, within range of passing youngsters, were photos of sexual intercourse, bodily excretions, and perversions including sodomy and bestiality.

I read accounts of underground films—called "snuff" movies—that showed actual tortures and murders.

Entertainment had reached the ultimate end. People were being killed for the camera!

There was even evidence, reported in a book called *The Ultimate Evil* (by Maury Terry), that the famous Son of Sam murders were related to grotesque films produced by practicing Satanists.

Flipping around the cable channels, I came across a talk show featuring harlots giving sexual advice. The show's producer hated Catholicism with such vehemence that he had himself filmed in front of a Manhattan church screaming blasphemies about the Virgin Mary.

At just about every newsstand was a weekly paper that advertised the services of call-girls, now so bold as to accept credit cards; and when I walked into an occult bookstore to see what *that* was all about, I noticed they sold the Satanic Bible. (The clerks, busy stuffing hundreds of books into envelopes, looked alarmed at my presence and quickly shooed me away.)

And the evil was graduating. What had once been confined to nudie magazines was now pervading mainstream magazines and newspapers. Risque photos and open talk of sex were beginning to find their way into *Time* and *Newsweek.* It was like a plague. Soon *Cosmopolitan* would be turned into a female version of *Penthouse*, with explicit sex surveys and a pull-out section on astrology.

Sex and the occult: a potent combination. If you study the history of occultism, it has always involved sexual acts as well as drug use and the sacrifice of innocents. By that definition cities like San Francisco and New York had become a huge and collective center of sophisticated witchcraft. According to one report, so prevalent was violent sex among homosexuals that workshops were offered on how to engage in sado-masochism without causing permanent disfigurement.

Abortion mills advertise in the Manhattan subways, along with gypsy fortunetellers or horoscope readers; and in Greenwich Village "gay" couples hold hands and kiss openly on the streets, part of a gigantic and domineering homosexual subculture that is now carrying around the HIV virus in fulfillment of another LaSalette prophecy which warned of *"infectious diseases"* and *"plagues."*

By April of 1993 the New York City Health Department would estimate up to 200,000 people in New York *alone* were infected with the HIV virus while another 39,700 adult males had already developed the AIDS disease.

I know this is a very unpleasant topic, but many of the homosexuals, frequenters of bars like the Hellfire, also carried hepatitis A and B viruses or parasitic infections such as amebiasis, lamblia, giardiasis, and shigellosis, the result of certain perverse and unsanitary activities, which, ironically, are also common to Satanists.

CHAPTER 13

Face of the Warrior

I started to shut out New York, reading Scripture and praying alone in my Manhattan apartment. *"Advance against Satan by means of prayer,"* Our Lady of Medjugorje had said. *"Put on the armor for battle and with the rosary in your hand defeat him!"*

Despite the initial fear, there was no longer any doubt in my mind that with prayer demons could be deactivated, and great graces flowed like living water sent from the heavenlies.

How beautiful this all was to me. I saw little miracles everywhere. Slowly but surely, instead of feeling aggravated with people, which happens to you in New York, I realized I needed to love and have patience. Everyone was worthy of love. Even the greatest sinners. For they were often victims of invisible realities.

Evil was not just at the underside of New York. It wasn't just in Times Square or a crackhouse on Avenue B. I now began to see the evil of everyday life. It rode in the limousines with yuppies splurging after another hit with junk bonds, and it strode alongside millionaires walking their poodles near Central Park.

All around the city an anonymous artist had spraypainted macabre black silhouettes on sidewalks, highway abutments, and the sides of tenement buildings—as if he too sensed the invisible and sinister presence.

I wasn't going to ignore evil or compromise with it any longer. I heeded what was said at Fatima, where Lucia emphasized that "from now on we must choose sides. Either we are for God or we are for the devil. There is no other possibility."

I broke up with a woman who insisted that Jesus was just a "carpenter," and I noticed the puzzled and maybe even appalled look on the face of another woman I dated when I showed her my statue of the Archangel Michael.

I'm sure she thought I was crazy. I also gave this woman a picture of the Shroud of Turin, and even though, as a professional model, she was about as worldly as a woman can get, she immediately associated the image with Jesus.

Such is the power of the Shroud. Most of you know what that is, the incredible image of a tall muscular man that was miraculously inflected on a length of ancient linen cloth.

There have always been disputes about the shroud. There are those who say the cloth was Christ's burial shroud while others, mainly agnostic or atheistic scientists, argue that it dates back only six centuries.

I've dealt with many scientists, and I know that to them *everything* is a controversy. They still don't agree on many basic aspects of human biology, and they even argue about what powers the sun.

Like the legal profession, science has suffocated itself in minutiae, taking rules of evidence to the extreme. All the intricacies have boggled their minds and narrowed their views to the point where they can't see beyond their own microscopes. Most scientists, I began to realize, possess less of the truth than those little old Irish ladies who sat through noon Mass at Our Lady of Good Counsel Church.

Those who are debunkers of God serve as foot soldiers for Satan.

How much do they really know, these folks who lead us to believe they're unfolding the great mysteries of the cosmos?

They now say one of the major components of the universe is something called "dark matter." This is a new discovery.

What is "dark matter"?

According to *The New York Times,* it's "invisible matter of an unknown kind."

I was frequently in touch with scientists, and they treated belief in *anything* supernatural as a relic of superstition. This is precisely what Satan wants them to say. They don't believe in God and think the devil is an idiotic archetype, what you might call an anachronism—a cultural leftover from primitive times. Evil spirits are the stuff of witch doctors and aborigines!

The only reality is that which can be perceived by the very limited human faculties. The only reality is the reality you can taste, touch, hear, and see.

Nothing exists if it can't be proven statistically or seen through an electron microscope. It's materialism taken to the point of absurdity. The concept of a supernatural messiah called Christ doesn't fit into their view of a mechanical universe, and neither does the Shroud. Certainly not the Shroud. Scientists seem to hate that thing. Later, when they claimed it could not be Christ's burial cloth because their dating showed it to be a mere 600 years old, I chuckled to myself, for there have been cases where they've dated the shells of live snails to be 26,000 years old, or a recently killed seal to be 1,300. When I visited with Richard Leakey, the fossil hunter in Nairobi, Kenya, I saw one instance (with a famous skull called "1470") where their dating techniques had been off by a million years!

I knew science pretended to know more than it did, and even if the dating *was* right in the case of the Shroud and it *isn't* the actual burial shroud, the key question is how the image got onto the cloth in the first place.

Clearly it is not pigment nor any form of etching, burn mark, or paint.

More to the point, I felt tremendous spiritual uplifting and protection from pictures of the Shroud. I carried them with me everywhere around Manhattan, and a 7-by-8-inch glossy of the Shroud took its place at the centers of my living room and bedroom.

At times, while deep in prayer, bothered by the turmoil around me, oppressed by the sights and sounds of New York, I would glance at it, and the picture seemed to *radiate*.

I'm convinced it's a miraculous image, no matter what the radiocarbon dating says. This was a tough guy, a tough and yet somehow gentle and enormously kind man, this guy on the Shroud—not so much tough as *strong*. In the long features and short beard is the presence and wisdom of God.

I also felt the peaceful grace of angels. I remember praying on my couch one Sunday afternoon when suddenly, my eyes closed, I bolted up because for a split second I "saw" a huge towering entity lean into my field of "vision" for just a moment. Tall and brilliant white. The figure had wings and edged just within range of my right perception.

Those experiences more than made up for the harassment by demons, for there were several times, deep in prayer, when I felt an actual *punch*.

I heard strange knocks on the walls. I was interrupted during contemplation.

There were times invisible forces tried to frighten me by making me feel like I had claws digging into my heart.

I just kept praying. When we're in the grace of prayer, there is an interior strength and radiance. *"Whoever listens to me will dwell safely,"* says the Lord (*Proverbs* 1:33), *"and will be secure without fear of evil."*

Prayer and holy objects also discourage evil attack. I remember getting another important relic, a picture of the Virgin of Guadalupe and quickly this miraculous image took a place on a makeshift altar in my bedroom, next to the Shroud.

Mary, bowing slightly, looking downward with tenderness. Mary, my mother, our mother, calling us now to the side of her Son, the ultimate *prayer-warrior,* at a crucial juncture in history.

CHAPTER 14

Lucifer Rising

It's crucial because Satan has enhanced his aggression knowing his time is short. He has always been around, but he is now more pervasive. He pervaded Communist countries during the first half of the century and began pervading America, through its popular culture, in the Sixties, Seventies, and Eighties.

Lucifer was in our very midst, fallen to earth (*Luke* 10:18) before the beginning of time, the "morning star," now prince of pride; and he sought above all to engender rebellion.

It was Satan who aspired to God's very seat and the 1960s initiated a truly epic era of disorder and godlessness.

It is no wonder that the Apostle Paul (*Ephesians* 2:2) identified Satan as "prince of the power of the air." New music unlike any previous music blared from radios and stereos. Swaying to the beat, young people rejected the values of their parents and for that matter rejected the values of Judeo-Christianity, which was really what the revolution was about.

"Down to the netherworld your pomp is brought, the music of your harps," says *Isaiah* 14:11-15. *"The couch beneath you is the maggot, your covering, the worm. How have you fallen from the heavens, O morning star, son of the dawn!"*

Everything seemed to be in upheaval. There was Vietnam and hippies and political assassinations. There was Timothy Leary, a Luciferian, and the lingering shadow, the huge oppressive cloud, of Freud and Darwin.

There was *Time* Magazine with a cover story on April 8, 1966, that asked, "Is God Dead?"

I went to high school and then college during the 1960s and 1970s, and along with most of my classmates I bought Darwinism and flirted with agnosticism. The books we read were by negativists like Sartre or Pierre de Chardin, who either disavowed God or purveyed the idea of an impersonal Creator: sort of God-as-energy-and-matter, "soul of the earth," a concept that paved the way to the "New Age," which English occultist Aleister "The Beast" Crowley, whose own mother thought he was an anti-christ, had announced back in 1900, at the very onset of our century.

Crowley conducted sex rituals, promoted drugs, and extolled the virtues of sodomy as he traveled from London to Cairo and finally on to the United States. He was the forerunner of American hedonism and debauchery. It was as if he'd cursed the Western Hemisphere. "Be strong, O man! lust, enjoy all things of sense and rapture," wrote Crowley, who died just before the Sixties and drew inspiration from Harpakrad, a Greek-Egyptian pagan god and one of the forces that he said were "ruling this world at present."

This occultism filled the minds of many young musicians, and in turn they filled the air of our dormitories with their sorcery. Jim Morrison, Janis Joplin, Jimi Hendrix. Don't get me wrong. Not all the music was bad. I loved a lot of it and still do. But much of it was raucous, it was rebellious, it captured you with its undulating, seductive rhythms, and it promoted sex, drugs, and lust of all kinds, which just happened to be Crowley's agenda.

Hendrix complained at one point that the devil was trying to possess him, and both he and Joplin were soon dead of drug overdoses.

Most musicians didn't realize what was going on, but there is no denying the spiritual dimension. An unseen force was often at work and there *were* a few who sensed it. Fretted guitarist Jerry Garcia of the Grateful Dead,

"Maybe we're opening doors for some demons from the ninth dimension or something."

Until 1966 the Grateful Dead were known as The Warlocks.

That was also the year that the Church of Satan was founded by one of Crowley's spiritual sons, Anton Szandor LaVey. On April 30, 1966 (known to pagans as Walpurgis Night), LaVey stepped out of his hellish black house in San Francisco and, eyes of amber aglare, officially declared the "Age of Satan."

The photo of someone who closely resembled a demon, a Satanist wearing a mask, found its way onto the cover of a mysterious album containing a hit called "Hotel California." The song, about a hotel that you can check into but can never leave, carried a number of occult innuendoes and made references to 1969, a year that saw a particularly powerful surge of occultic evil, including the Manson murders, the publication of LaVey's Satanic Bible, and birth of the gay-rights movement (when homosexuals at an after-hours bar on Christopher Street in Greenwich Village rebelled against a police raid).

That same year there was also a horrible riot during a concert at Altamont Speedway just outside of San Francisco, provoked by a motorcycle gang called Hell's Angels. Five people were killed and much of the turmoil erupted while the Rolling Stones were onstage singing a spellbinding invocation called "Sympathy for the Devil."

Then there were the Doors, a group led by the spooky young poet-musician named Jim Morrison who, during one concert, grasped a lamb to his chest as if conquering it.

In 1970 Morrison, who claimed he was possessed by the spirit of an Indian, married a high priestess from a Celtic coven and at the *wiccan* ceremony drew blood and drank it with "consecrated" wine.

Soon afterward Morrison too was dead, succumbing in Paris at the age of 27.

Elvis? He was a devoted follower of another famed occultist named Madame Blavatsky. Presley even quoted her from the stage. Accused of black magic, Blavatsky had been a trance medium who claimed to be in touch with hidden

Tibetan "masters" and formed her beliefs into the occult religion of Theosophy, which incorporated spirit communication with concepts of reincarnation. She was the female counterpart of Crowley and her apparitions were of the goddess Isis, another pagan idol. Included in her mystical brooch was a swastika and hexagram. Blavatsky's seminal work was *The Secret Doctrine,* a book of "ageless wisdom." That was what plagued poor Elvis.

The same "ageless wisdom" also ensnared John Lennon. Along with wife Yoko Ono, Lennon regularly consulted a network of psychics, Tarot-card readers, and spiritists. They attended seances at their apartment in the Dakota, and had mediums stop by to perform their magic in their very living room.

Elvis died of drugs or food-poisoning in 1977, while Lennon was killed on December 8, 1980, by a maniacal young gunman, Mark David Chapman, who claimed to be possessed by seven demons.

The devil's track marks could be spotted from Woodstock to Monterey. Musicians appeared onstage wearing the ankh, a pagan cross with a loop on the top, or the "peace symbol," the bent, upside-down cross in a circle, Athough I didn't know it at the time (thinking it just the emblem of pacifism), the peace symbol is also known as the "cross of Nero" and, as the arms of the cross are broken, is used by occultists, including satanic ritualists, to represent the defeat of Christianity.

So preoccupied with The Beast was a guitarist named Jimmy Page that he actually purchased Boleskine House, Crowley's old country residence, which is located on the shore of Loch Ness in Scotland.

No surprise, then, that when one of Zeppelin's songs, "Stairway to Heaven," was played in reverse, the words to emerge from the slur of backward-masking were, "Here's to my sweet Satan."

As for the Rolling Stones, there were published rumors that a Swedish model associated with the group was spotted storing dried human parts for magic rituals, and at the band's periphery was also an avant-garde filmmaker named Kenneth Anger who wanted to cast Mick Jagger in a movie called *Lucifer Rising.*

CHAPTER 15

Pure Danger

A spirit was moving in the West, a spirit less obvious than the satanic spirit of Nazis and Communists—a touch less blatant than the Red Dragon of Mao—but in some ways a spirit that was as pervasive and threatening.

While in Russia the devil dragged souls to Hell through atheism, in the West he did the same through crime, lust, materialism, and paganism.

You've now run across the term "pagan" several times, and let's make sure we all understand what we're talking about. By current definition a pagan is someone who is polytheistic—worshipping more than one God, or worshipping a non-personal or demonic "god." A demonic god or creature-like spirit would represent Satan or his demons. Ancient Greeks, Romans, and Egyptians were pagans, as were many American Indians. They revered nature spirits, gods of the water and earth and air. Gods of wind and rain. Sun gods. Gods other than the Lord of the Old and New Testaments.

Egyptians were probably the most sophisticated of the ancient pagans. They built huge pyramids and temples deifying humans, and their gods included Osiris, the spirit of vegetation, and Horus, the god of heaven. There were also female deities such as Isis (who was the mother of Horus) and gods or goddesses of the sky.

That was back 5,000 years ago. Even before then, European cavemen known as Cro-Magnon left cave art exhibiting the same kind of superstition: etched pictures of strange-looking creatures with human bodies but animal heads, really evil spirits. In *Ezekiel* (8:10-18) we see that ancient Israelites provoked God's wrath by "worshipping the sun toward the east." The very first of the Commandments (*Exodus* 20:2-5) warns, *"I am the Lord your God, who brought you out of the land of Egypt, out of the house of bondage. You shall have no other gods before me."*

During the Roman Empire, which came after the pyramids, there were gods such as Jupiter, Juno, and Vesta. There were also hundreds of lesser gods, including a god of gold coins. Christianity replaced the pagan religion of Rome by A.D. 380, but paganism still flourished in Africa, the South Pacific, and the Americas, where Indians sacrificed humans or ingested buttons of peyote to come into contact with nature spirits.

Like Egyptians, American Indians used charms and magic rituals to get what they wanted, and they also built pyramids on their "sacred" areas. Many are baffled at how both Egyptians and South American Indians, separated by a 3,000-mile-wide ocean, got the idea to build pyramids around the same time. They also wonder how widely separated civilizations, from Mesopotamia to the Pacific, all came to use the swastika, which is a pagan "sun sign," as a magical emblem. I believe it's fairly easy to explain: their inspiration came from demons. Take a look at a totem pole and the grotesque images that are supposed to represent the various Indian "deities."

Many gods or goddesses were represented in the form of animals like the snake (which since *Genesis* has symbolized the devil) while others were depicted with horns. In Nordic regions there were gods of war, gods of thunder, gods of destruction. In Africa, especially in areas where *juju* is practiced, there are so many gods they are beyond count. They are summoned through mysterious and often bloody rituals in which roosters, leopards, and even humans are sacrificed.

This is sorcery. This is idolatry. We are told (*Psalms*

96:5) that "all the gods of the peoples are idols," and that idolatry (*1 Corinthians* 10:20) is "sacrifice to demons." In *Revelation* 22:15, sorcerers and idolaters are lumped with murderers and the sexually immoral.

In Europe, paganism took the form of Masonry and witchcraft, both of which borrow from Egyptian rituals, while in America it manifested first as old-fashioned witchcraft but later as spiritualism, psychic phenomena, and then the New Age.

Currently it is manifesting itself as goddess worship and occult energies of the "universe."

While most pagans are not really aware that they are tapping into demonic forces, when they *are* fully aware, when they contact demons knowingly, we call it Satanism.

Satanists, too, revere nature spirits and make no bones about their reverence for Lucifer, prince of the earthly spirits.

Like Haitians, who call it voodoo, Satanists borrow heavily from old Egyptian or Central African rituals that involve blood. To the Satanist, as to witches and New Agers, *"self"* is the highest embodiment of human life and man is his own god. According to Anton LaVey, Satanism is "essentially a human potential movement."

During the 1960s and 1970s, paganism began afflicting the entire culture of the United States. It's never pleasant to dwell on the negative, and I must warn you not to become obsessed with evil. I don't enjoy writing about it, and while I must name certain names, it isn't my place to judge or condemn. I have my own failings.

But as I said, to win a war we must know the enemy. And one thing I learned was that paganism and the satanic have permeated our culture, whether music, religion, or movies. Take for example *Rosemary's Baby,* the film about a group of Satanists who use a woman (Mia Farrow) to breed the devil's child.

Rosemary's Baby was directed by Roman Polanski and filmed inside the Dakota—the same famous, malevolent-looking building where John Lennon was shot. *Rosemary's Baby* was a blockbuster when I was in high school and was based on the activities of people like America's chief satanist, Anton LaVey, who made public appearances including on *Donahue* and Johnny Carson's *Tonight Show,* where he performed a ritual summoning success for the show.

Pure danger. One of LaVey's early followers was Susan "Sadie" Atkins, who later joined the notorious Manson Family and was arrested for the sensational 1969 killing of actress Sharon Tate—who was married to Polanski.

Manson himself was linked to a second satanic church known as "The Process" and studied the occult religion of Scientology. His followers swore that Manson could bring a dead animal to life and had extraordinary powers of ESP. Manson's quest to kill was inspired in part by a song called "Helter Skelter," which, coming full circle, was written by John Lennon.

A megalomaniac, Manson declared he was the incarnation of both the devil and Jesus, or the "universal mind," a term that later came into prominence in the New Age Movement.

Like shamans and witches, like LaVey and Crowley, Manson was into sexual magic, drug rituals, and reverence for nature spirits.

His eyes exuded pure malice and even his name is curious, for when you reverse it, when you take "Manson" backwards (as Satanists often reverse words that are holy), you get something akin to the sacred title of Jesus, "Son of Man."

*The statue of Our Lady at
St. Patrick's Cathedral
in New York.*

St. Michael the Archangel

85

Tarot cards, crystals, hallucinogenic drugs, and parapsychology are all elements of the "New Age" culture.

The Shroud of Turin

Sister Lucia, the only Fatima visionary still living.

The miracle of the Bleeding Host
in Betania, Venezuela.

Solar phenomena, such as this occurrence
at Betania, are common at Marian apparition sites.

Pope Paul VI

Pope John Paul II
89

As man-made and natural disasters such as war, abortion, famine, drought, volcano eruption, floods and hurricanes increase...

90

. . . attendance at prayer services, such as this ecumenical prayer service called by the Pope, and Mass attendance, such as at St. James in Medjugorje, has also increased.

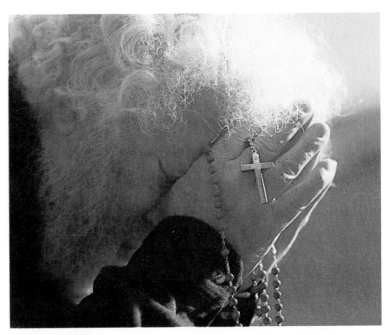

Prayer Warriors
92

Mother Teresa's humbling ability to radiate Christ to all she meets is the goal of every prayer warrior.

Jacinta, Lucia and Francisco in 1917, received specific warnings from Our Lady regarding Russia.

The Pope, in spiritual union with all bishops, consecrates the world to the Immaculate Heart of Mary, May 13, 1982.

Ukrainian visionary Josyp Terelya received messages from the Blessed Virgin regarding his homeland.

Chernobyl nuclear accident site.

Medjugorje visionary Vicka with author Michael Brown.

St. James Church, 1993, devoid of pilgrims.

St. James Church crowded with pilgrims before the war.

City of Mostar, in former Yugoslavia, devastated by war.

The remains of Saints Peter and Paul Church in Mostar.

*Individual and group prayer are
more powerful than evil in the world.*

BLOOD TIMES VIDEO

for
EXORCIST!
CURSE
of the DEVIL

The miraculous picture of Our Lady of Quito, Ecuador.

CHAPTER 16

A Man of Wealth and Taste

"Children, darkness reigns over the whole world. Satan is working hard in the world. This is the time of the devil." Mary was apparently saying that at Medjugorje, but we weren't getting her messages, not in the common press, not even from the pulpit. Satan, she warned, was *"lurking for each individual"* (September 4, 1986) and filling our eyes and ears with confusion and most importantly temptation. The devil had a plan, the Virgin warned, a tremendous plan that was not apparent to us.

A plan that involved not just the practices of paganism but the way our entire society functions. As he had in France during the 19th century, Satan sought to entirely secularize our nation—take God out of all civil life, under the guise of human liberties and "separation of church and state." Satan used that principle—which originally was intended to protect the *Church* from the *state,* not the reverse!—to divorce any form of religious observance from the public arena.

Thus a country founded on the principle of "one nation under God," a nation discovered by an explorer whose very ship had been called the *Santa Maria,* was becoming a nation of *many* gods.

You couldn't have a nativity scene in front of the town

hall, but the spookier the better when it came to the devil's day, Halloween.

Satan's greatest success had been in dominating godless, totalitarian governments, but it was difficult to do that in America so he focused on those institutions which are largely out of direct democratic control: universities, bureaucracies, courtrooms, scientific laboratories, and most especially the media.

One nation under God was now a place that wouldn't even acknowledge His existence.

God meant suffering, self-sacrifice, the narrow road. Satan was the rich and lenient uncle who only wanted you to have a good time. It was a new age, the age of self, an age in which we could forget our old Christian guilt and "hang-ups."

God was a cop-out. God was an anachronism. Now that we knew what caused earthquakes, and the sun to rise, now that we knew how lightning formed, now that we knew so many secrets of nature—there was no need for an old anthropomorphic God with a white beard.

Now, if we wanted to believe in God, said our scientists, we had to think in terms of a celestial cloud—hydrogen and carbon.

While the previous decades had witnessed Satan operating in crude ways—starting wars, gassing Jews, instituting Communism and nuclear weapons—the 1970s saw Lucifer grow more subtle, indirect, and sophisticated. He was what Mick Jagger described as a man of wealth and taste. His initial offensive was a bit vulgar, but now that he had grabbed a huge chunk of Judeo-Christian America he could polish his act and blend into the scenery.

Refined. The devil was becoming more refined and thus was able to slip into many more circumstances. He was no longer just an Aleister Crowley or a Russian hooligan or a Charles Manson. Now he wore a well-pressed suit or the trendy denim of a professor.

He was a criminal one moment, a cop, lawyer, or judge the next. He played both sides of the law. Some of his evil was of an illegal nature, but much of it was allowed by an increasingly liberal justice system.

Robe flowing, gavel in hand, he stood over a Supreme Court that legalized abortion on January 22, 1973.

That heinous decision added another important component of witchcraft to American culture—blood sacrifice. Now, in addition to the rituals of drugs *(pharmakeia),* sex *(saturnalia),* and music (to a voodoo beat), we had a massive sacrifice of innocents.

In 1970, 600,000 abortions. By 1975, a million. By 1990, 1.6 million a year in America alone, and another 35 million around the world, which meant that each year five times as many were slaughtered as in all the years of the Nazi Holocaust.

Now witchcraft was incorporated into the populace at large, with astrology columns in more than 1,200 American newspapers, and instead of a cauldron, instead of Yoruba drums, we had movies, the stereo, and television.

One of the hit TV shows was called *Bewitched.*

So yes, Satan is a ritualist. He also became a counselor and a therapist. He spoke about "sexual freedom" and everybody's own "space." He took the human-potential movement out of LaVey's "church" and incorporated it into pop psychology. Soon it would even enter evangelical prosperity sermons.

His real goal, of course, was not freedom or self-improvement but enslavement to loveless sensuality. His real goal was to eradicate marriage and replace it with "living together"—fornication. Now even adultery was something that a hefty percentage of Americans indulged in. More than a quarter of the married men admitted to it.

People were even proud to call themselves homosexuals (there was now a thing called "gay pride"), and sodomy, which had been very important to people like Crowley, became a human "right."

Putting on his scientist's smock, Satan tinkered with the very stuff of life: artificial fertilization and DNA.

Man was becoming his own creator.

While the Church became embroiled in modernism, or was attacked by disaffected Catholics who'd started their own unaffiliated congregations, science and the secular press, full of aging hippies, were gaining tremendous momentum. The new literary lion was a strange novelist from New York who had once stabbed his own wife, while the media's hero at the cinema was a short, frumpy, and paranoid comedian who showed little but disdain for religion, mocking it as if it were an exercise in mental illness. At the same time *he* was himself undergoing years of psychotherapy—and would one day be caught with his girlfriend's daughter in an outrageous sex scandal. When the first Earth Day had come around in April of 1970 it had little to do with human welfare and was hosted by a New Age guru named Ira Einhorn who was known as "the Unicorn" and was arrested for the murder of his girlfriend, Holly Maddux, whose body was found in a trunk on the porch of the Unicorn's apartment.

Hero of the liberals, Einhorn was also friendly with the growing legion of psychics. There were spoon-benders. There were clairvoyants. There were love signs and people talking to philodendra.

Now you could even call a radio show, or soon a 900 number, and get a horoscope or psychic reading.

Scientists at one of America's most prestigious "think-tanks," Stanford Research Institute, were testing Israeli psychic Uri Geller, and so rampant was the occult behind the Iron Curtain that a report on witches and psychics there was circulated within the U.S. Defense Intelligence Agency.

Along with the outpouring of occultism came bizarre reports of UFOs and flying-saucer "abductions." As Dr. Nelson S. Pacheco, a mathematician who worked for the Air Force, points out, the UFO sightings of the 1960s soon gave way to an outbreak of mysterious crop formations and cattle mutilations in the 1970s and 1980s. "Both the cattle mutilations and the crop-circle reports were often accompanied by strange lights reminiscent of the more classical UFO phenomenon," says Pacheco, who believes UFOs are a demonic phenomenon—a deception that is often linked to satanic activity. Indeed, there are indications that victims of satanic ritualism have encountered the same little "men" as UFO buffs. Demons in masquerade?

Yes, however bizarre it sounds, however difficult to pull together in our unexpecting finite minds, there was a massive infusion of eerie phenomena. I believe much of it was a sign of the demonic entities that, as Pope Leo supposedly foresaw, as Our Lady of LaSalette warned, were pouring into our earthly domain.

"The coming of the lawless one is according to the working of Satan, with all power, signs, and lying wonders," said the Apostle Paul (*Thessalonians* 2:9-12). "And with all unrighteous deceptions among those who perish, because they did not receive the love of the truth, that they might be saved. And for this reason God will send them strong delusion, that they should believe the lie, that they all may be condemned who did not believe the truth but had pleasure in unrighteousness."

Mankind, specifically Western society, was on a binge of insubordination, and this itself was a hidden aspect of occultism, for rebellion, it says in *Samuel* 15:23; "is as the sin of witchcraft."

"Beware," warns Paul in *Colossians* 2:8, "lest anyone cheat you through philosophy and empty deceit..."

Playboy! Penthouse! The joy of drugs! The sexual revolution! Suddenly sex, especially illicit intercourse, was in the open and everywhere. There was incredible pressure on young people to shake loose of their old virginal "hang-ups." Linda Lovelace, a porn star, became an overnight sensation. Theaters which once showed respectable movies, or had been Broadway stages, now showed movies like *Behind the Green Door* or *The Devil and Miss Jones*—hardcore films that often had satanic inferences woven into the vacant scenery.

The star of *Behind the Green Door* was none other than Marilyn Chambers, a model who had once been the wholesome-looking woman holding a baby on boxes of Ivory Snow detergent.

Was it a coincidence that one of the major X-rated film directors was named "Damiano," which approximates demon in Greek? Was it coincidence that the new sex practices were ones formerly confined to rituals of sex magic? Was it a coincidence that a key proponent of sodomy had been the occultist Aleister Crowley, who was a demigod to the American counterculture? A deluge of pornography led young couples to begin indulging in practices that were formerly taboo, and to begin using abortion as birth control.

Meanwhile "yippies" were on the loose. There were "love-ins." There was the Chicago Seven. When one of them, Jerry Rubin, visited Fordham University, I remember him lighting a marijuana joint up there at the microphone, and we were also graced with a visit by Abbie Hoffman, who'd written a book aptly entitled *Revolution for the Hell of It*.

The age of hellishness. Satan was instituting liberalized laws, godless philosophy, occult books, horror films, a rebellious press, and unending TV violence. Hollywood now glorified the Mafia and with *A Clockwork Orange* took violence to new, blood-curdling heights. It also began promoting liberal politics.

The cinema was wedded to revolution; Jane Fonda married Tom Hayden.

The rest of America was suffering "future shock" and escaping into space odysseys. The big Broadway show was *Jesus Christ Superstar,* which depicted Christ as a forlorn hippie. He was now just one of us. Blue jeans. Tattered blue jeans and long, unkempt hair. That was the symbol of my college era. Hair, mustaches, long bushy sideburns, beards. I was never a hippie, but my hair curled down to my collar and a mustache sprouted—anything to look different from the "straight" old coots who wore suits and still lived orderly, God-fearing lives.

Everything was suddenly okay. Fornication was fine, said the new sex researchers. Everyone was doing it. Faithfulness and virginity? They were relics of the Victorian Age. I remember my college girlfriend reading a bestseller called *Open Marriage* which in essence endorsed adultery.

Freud was king. He told us that sex is the all-important factor in life, that it shapes all that we are, and that if we have emotional or spiritual problems these can all be blamed on someone else, or on emotions we can't control.

There was no more sin. There were only "hang-ups" and "aberrations." Anything wrong was okay because it wasn't our doing. Blame it on environment or genes. I'm okay, you're okay. Everything was okay. We could be excused for anything, including rape and murder. Criminals were suddenly treated as if *they* were the ones suffering an injustice. Yet at the same time the "intelligentsia" espoused "humanism" they were dehumanizing all of us. There was a terrific loss of human dignity. When I went to school the most prominent psychologist was an atheistic behaviorist named B. F. Skinner who proposed putting people in training boxes like those used to experiment with rats.

Man, we were told, is nothing more than a highly evolved mammal, and like an animal we have no real control of our emotions and no real soul, and with no soul there is no afterlife. We are just a bunch of instincts. The soul is an archaic belief invented because humans fear death. And with that, with those beliefs, psychology began promoting what Crowley had promoted: lust ye all, live only for today!

And step on whoever gets in your way.

It was an extraordinary outbreak of selfishness. The stage was set for Wall Street and the "Me Generation." Rebellion, rebellion everywhere. Everyone was rebelling against something. Mostly we were expected to rebel against what our parents said. There were Germaine Greer and Betty Freidan sowing the seeds of radical feminism, and soon Satan would join radical feminists with the free-sex and pro-abortion movements. Soon it would also become a cover for lesbianism.

The sexes blurred—men and women wore many of the same clothes, including work boots—and homosexuality became an exciting experimentation. Some men and women, the transsexuals, went so far as to have surgeons physiologically change their gender, which in older and wiser times was called self-mutilation.

In the political arena kids were carrying Communist flags and extolling the Chinese tyrant Mao Tse-Tung, whose banner bore a red dragon.

Yes, Satan wasn't quite as refined as he was to become, but everywhere one looked he was planting his insidious seeds. One day the blatant drug use would be refined into cocaine. One day the riotous sex would be institutionalized by psychologists and sex therapists. One day fornication would be as natural as asking a girl to the prom. One day it would become *abnormal* for a woman older than twenty to be a virgin! One day the occult and black magic would be refined into parapsychology and the New Age Movement.

It was the age of Mahariji Mahesh Yogi. It was the Age of Aquarius. Everyone seemed to be "talking" to their plants, reading about Eastern or Amerindian magic, enrolling in Mind Control or Transcendental Meditation.

"Darkness reigns over the whole world...This is the time of the devil," Our Lady had said.

What just a few years before had been depicted in stark terms as evil in *The Exorcist,* or renounced by evangelists as occult, was now not only refined but so subtle and pervasive as to be virtually indistinguishable.

The occult became so commonplace that it wasn't considered the occult any longer.

The occult was good for you! By use of occult force, people in Scotland, at a place called Findhorn, were able to grow gigantic vegetables! Psychic power was the next stage of human evolution! The naked ape had ESP!

Especially hot on the bestseller list were books by an anthropologist named Carlos Castaneda who took drugs with Yaqui Indians and went on mental journeys that involved apparitions of spirit beings and magical animals—birds, insects, coyotes. I read nearly everything Castaneda wrote. It was fascinating. It struck a chord with my mystical interest. It was an incredible journey into a new dimension. Castaneda was taught by Indian sorcerers how to mind-travel and "see" another reality. He hung around Yaqui sorcerers who plied him with hallucinogenic drugs like *yerba del diablo* and peyote. He had out-of-body experiences and communed with spiritual entities that were called "allies." I found it heady stuff. It was remarkable to delve into such a dimension. A new reality!

What I didn't know and what I never would have accepted, back when I was fresh out of college, is that the magical creatures that Castaneda wrote about—the forces his gurus invoked—are in reality demons.

CHAPTER 17

The First Prayer of the Warrior

It was thus no surprise that people in my generation were confused and harbored an unhealthy interest, as I had, in things like psychic phenomena. This was the world we were in. This is what the young of my generation—the baby-boomers—suddenly faced. This is what we watched as Western society began to unravel. Back in my college days there were drugs everywhere. Speed. Peyote. LSD. I recall one fellow "flipping out" in the dorms and screaming (like Hendrix) that the devil was after him.

Maybe he was. Maybe, in a drugged state, the human spirit is open to demonic infestation.

I don't attribute *everything* to demons. I don't dismiss everything about psychiatry. No doubt a number of problems in the thought process have behavioral or biochemical roots. The same with illness: there are good genes and there are bad genes.

But my point is that evil spirits exist, and their influence is far greater than our materialistic, worldly, and "rationalistic" society realizes. They cause the blindness and oppression. That's why they call them "forces of dark." They try to discourage us and cloud if not totally obscure our vision. Or they hook us to obsession. We become obsessed with money, emotional hurts, relationships, sexual tendencies, work, superstitions, and people in general. That's why Heaven is now intervening. That's why Our Blessed Mother is appearing on earth. The Holy Spirit has sent Mary, and possibly fundamentalism and the charismatic renewel as well, as beacons in the spiritual darkness.

The Holy Spirit! I could *feel* Him. How I grew to love that member of the Trinity! He responds so directly to us. *Come Holy Spirit.* I would say that dozens of times, hundreds of times, from the heart and mind together, and I could feel His sweet Grace flowing into my spirit.

Sweet. Grace is sweet. It isn't sweet like chocolate is sweet but ethereal and *heavenly* sweet.

And so easy to summon. *Come Holy Spirit.* When we pray, I learned right off, we have to enter into profound communication. Reciting novenas and other traditional prayers is an important avenue to grace, but we should never neglect the spontaneous aspect of supplications.

It is often when we are spontaneous, when we really send up heartfelt pleas, that our prayers pierce the clouds. God likes us to speak to Him as we speak to friends and neighbors. *Come Holy Spirit.* It is the prayer of guidance, and the prayer of protection. The Holy Spirit can break through any darkness, and He provides answers we could never think up ourselves.

Our most effective prayers are often those said when we least want to pray, or while we are in a state of depression or physical suffering.

The strongest prayers are often those said when it doesn't seem like God is listening.

At Medjugorje the Virgin has mentioned the Holy Spirit many times. She emphasizes spontaneity. She teaches prayer from the heart. While I was learning about the Holy Spirit and His wonders, the Virgin, I later discovered, was addressing Him directly to the children of Medjugorje. On March 28, 1985, she told them that in prayer we can find our way *"out of every situation that has no exit."*

"If you pray," said the Madonna of Medjugorje, *"Satan cannot defeat you, not even a little, because you are God's children and He is watching over you. Pray, and let the*

rosary always be in your hands as a sign to Satan that you belong to me."
And that you belong to the Spirit. For it is He who empowers Mary and sends her as a messenger. It's against Catholic teaching (Canon 1255 of Codex 1918) to adore Mary as we adore Christ. We venerate her and seek her assistance. When we do, the veneration redounds to the glory of the Trinity, just as Mary magnified God when Elizabeth (*Luke* 1:46) blessed her. It's clear from Scripture (*Revelation* 8:3) that the saints will intercede for us, and as far back as the fourth century—many, many centuries before anti-Catholics, working unwittingly with the forces of dissension, would besmirch the Virgin's role—Saint Chrysostom told us that, when under attack, we should fly to "the martyrs, the saints, and those who are pleasing to Him, and who have great power."

Our sacrifices and requests are purified through Mary, and with the Virgin comes instruction.

"Open your hearts to the Holy Spirit. Especially during these days the Holy Spirit is working through you. Open your hearts and surrender your life to Jesus," she said on May 23, 1985.

The most important thing in the spiritual life, says the Virgin, is to ask for the gift of the Holy Spirit. The Holy Spirit addresses all of our needs. We can ask the Spirit for discernment, we can ask the Holy Spirit to extend our vision, we can ask Him for health, and we can even ask the Holy Spirit how to *pray* to Him!

I found out quickly that the Holy Spirit is a better instructor than any book or preacher. *"Pray to the Holy Spirit for enlightenment."* He will lead us to where we should go for information and will help us choose the books to read. Passages from the Bible become more vivid and meaningful when they are read with His help. *Come Holy Spirit.*

Every prayer, especially in these treacherous times, is that much better if it begins with an invocation to the Holy Spirit. When the Holy Spirit comes, everything changes around us. It's the arrival of God's Spirit, the Spirit Jesus sent after His Resurrection. That's what to convert or to be "born again" means: arrival of the Holy Spirit.

Many people flock to sites of apparition to experience a

nearness to Christ and Mary, and there's no doubt in my mind that pilgrimages to authentic sites of apparition, especially those formally approved by the Church, offer special graces. Nor do I doubt that certain people, the so-called seers and visionaries, are granted greater visual access to heavenly entities.

But visionaries are no closer to God—and in many cases farther away—than those hidden little old ladies who for years have been invoking the Holy Spirit. The Spirit talks to all of us. He loves us as much as any seer. And He speaks to us every day in one form or another.

When we accept Him, when we have the Holy Spirit, we have the truth. When we have the Holy Spirit we are less likely to be deceived. The Spirit is truth (*1 John* 5:6) and when we have that, we are released from our errors and bondages. It is the Holy Spirit who illuminates and lifts our blindness. *"You shall know the truth,"* said Jesus (*John* 8:32), *"and the truth shall make you free."*

Thus do we see the importance of heartfelt prayer. *"Open your hearts to God like spring flowers which crave for the sun,"* the Virgin told a locutionist named Jelena at Medjugorje. *"When you pray, you are much more beautiful, like flowers, which after the snow, show all their beauty, and all their colors become indescribable."*

When asked, at Medjugorje, why she was so beautiful, the Virgin answered that it was because of how much she loves. The Holy Spirit surrounds us with attractiveness.

The more we pray, the more we receive the Holy Spirit. We must pray for His outpouring. We must pray for His constant manifestations. *"Come Holy Spirit. Come Holy Spirit and descend upon us. Come Holy Spirit and descend upon us as you did upon the first apostles!"*

With the Holy Spirit our spiritual blindness is cured and we see the true nature, or at least *part* of the true nature, of the spiritual world around us. We are granted a greatly enhanced sensitivity. We are better able to differentiate angels from deceiving spirits—and this is crucial, for the number of deceiving spirits seems virtually countless.

With the Holy Spirit we encounter angels because angels are *empowered* by the Spirit. They come through the Holy Spirit. They are created by the Holy Spirit. Just as we are created by the Spirit. That is what the Bible means by God breathing life into us. Life is the Spirit, a gift from the Lord because it is a part of the Lord. *"God is Spirit,"* Jesus told us *(John* 4:24), *"and those who worship Him must worship in spirit and truth."* Those who fail to see the reality of the Trinity are those we call materialists, and they are the ones, according to *Jude* (19), "who cause divisions, not having the Spirit."

Divisions. Jealousy. Envy. Materialism causes hatred and rancor, while the Holy Spirit grants us inner stability. It is no coincidence that Mary, promoter of the Holy Spirit, calls herself the Queen of Peace. At Medjugorje she tells the children that she herself prays to the Holy Spirit.

We feel the Spirit descend in a powerful but subtle bliss that takes us to heights of pleasure unlike any that can be afforded by the material world. What peace!

The weapons and shields, the equipment of battle, all lay in prayer, and prayer to the Holy Spirit is the first prayer of the prayer-warrior. It can't be emphasized enough how important it is to establish a relationship with the Paraclete. *"Begin by calling on the Holy Spirit each day,"* says Mary of Medjugorje. *"The most important thing is to pray to the Holy Spirit."*

Because when one has the Spirit, says Mary, *"one has everything."*

CHAPTER 18

Other Voices

Just as the Holy Spirit talks to us constantly, so does the devil. The difference is that evil speaks louder and more insistently. I must directly address that issue at this point: the influence and attributes of demons.

Where the Spirit is often a small still voice, the devil fills our brains with anxiousness, obsession, and animosities. I know this is the most controversial aspect of mysticism, the existence and power of demons. That's because Satan *wants* it to be controversial. He cannot stand the light. He does not want to be unmasked. Many people can accept God, and go so far as to accept Christ or the Blessed Virgin, maybe even angels, but will stop at the concept of actual evil entities. They consider that going too far. They consider that ''fundamentalism.'' They consider that Bible-thumping territory.

It also contradicts much of what we have been told by the modern ''science'' of psychology. While it's comfortable to think strictly in terms of psychological factors, doing so, explaining everything in psychological terms, is one of the great errors of our dark and confused century.

Many emotional disturbances, large and small, are provoked by evil spirits. These invisible and highly intelligent spirits whisper to us. They inflect ideas. They play upon our pride. They exaggerate differences and affronts. They instill egoism. They whisper about other people.

Listen to your thoughts. Take better note of the internal dialogue that moves through your mind like a computer punchtape.

The good thoughts, the thoughts that bring us clarity and peace—*lasting* peace—are from the Holy Spirit, while the unbalanced ones, the ones that instill oppression, pride, confusion and delusion, are temptations from the Evil One. He is always testing us. He is always sending us emotions that he hopes will lead to sin and misery. For reasons that will always remain a mystery, Satan has been granted the ability to tempt us every inch of the way. When we are at peace, he sends an unsettling thought. When we are mellow, hostility. When we are at rest, restlessness. When we feel holy, pride or lust. When we feel secure, anxiety.

Especially he sends egoism and spiritual pride. Our protection is the Holy Spirit.

Life is a constant battle between ideas sent to us by forces of both good and evil. It always comes down to free choice. It is up to us to choose *which* of the thoughts and emotions we want to maintain and nurture, along with which ones we want to act upon. When we allow ourselves to entertain and act upon the lustful thoughts, we disperse the Spirit and head toward sin. We become unsatisfied. We get restless. We fill our minds with dissatisfaction and jealousy. When we grasp and hold on to what is sent by Heaven, the result may be a difficult road, but it is a road that ends in exquisite bliss—if we hang on to it.

This is not to say that all thoughts are supernatural. No. Not at all. We have recognized the role of the brain since 600 B.C. Many of our thoughts are from our natural or psychological nature, a combination of memory, reasoning, and conditioning.

There are also urges which are a part of our human nature, the product of instincts.

But more thoughts than we realize are inspired by powers of evil. All of you have seen people who are kind and gentle one moment, full of hostility or irrationality the next. If it isn't a biochemical problem, or a simple personality disorder, it may well be something *spiritual* that plagues them. Our moods are frequently a product of the spiritual warfare. Light and dark are in constant battle over our personalities.

Yes, it's true; genes, food, and the environment—biochemical and behavioral factors—affect our thoughts. We all have certain "psychological" problems. Sunshine seems to put a smile on the face, while the wrong diet causes anxiety, depression, or hyperactivity.

Hormones can also play a role. There is no doubt about that. Our minds function through the brain, and since the brain is a physical organ, it is subject to physical influences. It may even be the case that certain toxic metals and hydrocarbons impair our mentalities.

But spirits can also be a factor, and this is more clearly seen in the extreme cases of "psychology." While the influence of evil is often hard to detect in lesser disorders like neurosis, which cause compulsions, obsessions, and phobias, it can become increasingly obvious with the degree of mental or emotional dysfunction. Let's take "psychosis" as an example. Psychosis can be organic, caused by paresis, tumors, or alcoholism. It's a state of tremendous psychological disorder, as is schizophrenia. Schizophrenia is a term that is normally used to describe a person who has delusions—delusions of persecution or grandeur—and even hallucinations. A schizophrenic can be very clever and bright, functioning with unimpaired intelligence, but there is a serious personality disorder in that person, sometimes causing the person to change moods to the point where the personality changes.

In extreme psychological episodes we see indications of "multiple personality." It means just what it says: a person who demonstrates not just mood swings but distinctly different personalities. The most famous cases were portrayed in books or movies such as *Sybil* and *The Three Faces of Eve.* So extreme are the different personalities that they often have completely different manners, styles, speech patterns, names, and even genders—male and female personalities in the same body! There are cases where a person lapses into various personalities and doesn't realize what he or she is doing when the secondary personality takes over. In some instances more than fifty personalities have been identified in a single person, personalities that are often unaware of the others.

In the case of Sybil we find an obsessive fear of Satan and in the case of Eve there were auditory hallucinations or "locutions"—both symptoms well known to those who study demonology.

Eve's rebellious alter-ego was demonstrated in poetry:

The laws of God, the laws of man,
He may keep that will and can;
Not I: let God and man decree
Laws for themselves and not for me.

My question is whether these other "personalities" are always the result of "psychological" agitation, or if, rather, they might be spiritual disturbances. In other words, some may well be the result of intrusion by familial and evil entities. When I was a newspaper reporter I interviewed a woman suffering this syndrome, and whether or not her main illness was *psychiatric* as opposed to *spiritual*, I do know for a fact that poltergeist phenomena were reported around her. She also demonstrated remarkable abilities at telepathy. This woman had at least three personalities, each with wholly different names. In many such cases only one of the personalities is aware of all the others—a controlling spirit. The rest of the personalities are in the dark. Perhaps this is what charismatics refer to as the "root demon."

Thus, it may be that many paranoids, hysterics, and schizoids are less in need of a psychiatrist than of a deliverance minister. I suspect this may have been true in the very case that spawned Freud's highly questionable theories of psychoanalysis. It was known as the case of "Anna O," the pseudonym given to a talented, highly cultured, and charitable yet exceedingly clever woman who was suffering serious and at times bizarre "mental" disturbances, including rapid mood shifts, mental lapses, somnolent episodes, and hallucinations. At times she could speak only French, at other times both French and Italian. Her syntax and grammar seemed to change, and she developed two distinctly different personalities, what Freud believed were the result of repressed emotions and sexuality.

"There were extremely rapid changes of mood leading

to excessive but quite temporary high spirits," wrote one of Freud's colleagues, Josef Breuer, "and at other times severe anxiety, stubborn opposition to every therapeutic effort and frightening hallucinations of black snakes, which was how she saw her hair, ribbons, and similar things...At moments when her mind was quite clear she would complain of the profound darkness in her head, of not being able to think, of becoming blind and deaf, of *having two selves, a real one and an evil one which forced her to behave badly* (my emphasis), and so on."

This woman had analyzed her own affliction better than either Freud or Breuer.

"...two selves, a real one and an evil one which forced her to behave badly..."

The poor woman also imagined that she was pregnant, writhing in cramps. They call this pseudocyesis, or "phantom pregnancy."

Although Breuer claimed to have cured her, Anna O suffered abnormalities long afterward.

According to Freud himself, the case seized Dr. Breuer with a "conventional horror" and ensnared the physician in an obsessive love-hate relationship. At one point, after hypnotizing Anna O, he fled the house in a cold sweat.

Does that sound like simple psychology?

Or had Freud and Breuer encountered a frightening, confusing, and ensnaring case of evil manifestation?

CHAPTER 19

The Nature of the Enemy

That's what evil does. It *ensnares* us. It draws us into its insidious web. It lies. It pretends. It exercises superb cleverness.

It can even pretend to be the voice of Jesus or Mary, granting us an immediate "peace" that soon enough transforms into confusion or division.

As the spiritual warfare has increased, as the demons pour in, they have greatly increased their annoyance and deceptions. This too is in fulfillment of prophecy. "During the time of the approach of the punishments announced at LaSalette, an unlimited number of false revelations will arise from Hell like a swarm of flies," warned mystic Marie Julie Jahenny in the 19th century, "a last attempt of Satan to choke and destroy the belief in the true revelations by false ones."

Just as there are psychological deceptions that fooled people like Freud, so too are there spiritual deceptions so refined that they have ensnared otherwise perceptive theologians—deceptions that expose themselves only to those who probe deeply and persistently. Such high-level deceptions bring to mind Magdalen of the Cross, a 16th-century nun in Cordova, Spain, who for 38 years managed to fool the greatest theologians in Spain as well as bishops and cardinals with false ecstasy, prophecy, levitation, and

119

even the stigmata. Toward the end of her life she had to undergo an exorcism.

Meanwhile Saint Catherine of Bologna experienced false apparitions of Our Lord and Blessed Mother for five years.

That's how clever evil is. Demons are shrewd because demons are super-intelligences. They have access to information we don't, and unnoticed, they have a field day. They masquerade and cover up. They twist the truth. They cause confusion and ultimately obsession and fright, as with Anna O.

They *ensnare* us until we are delivered of them.

Some of those who work in psychiatric wards will tell you that the only thing which causes an improvement in certain cases of psychosis is prayer—prayer of deliverance. Some of these people become "mentally ill" after committing grave sins such as murder and abortion or because they opened the spiritual door, the porthole of Hell, with drugs, alcoholism, prostitution, or occultic activities, including false revelation.

Often the point of entry is a damaged emotion, and it is for that reason that we can never judge a person. We can judge the sin, but not the person. We have no idea what burdens they secretly harbor, and so no matter what, we must treat the person with unconditional love. Everybody is born with some type of sinful proclivity. It might be a tendency to alcoholism, homosexuality, anger, addiction, sloth, or other things. We all have a cross. No one knows enough about evil spirits, but perhaps it is not always sin that attracts them but rather an emotional hurt or weakness, which is another reason not to judge. It is when a proclivity is allowed to grow due to our lack of discipline that we bear blame and fall into sin.

When we sin, God's grace is lessened. We have rejected the Spirit. And when there is no spiritual shield, evil spirits have easier access, striking at our soft spots. They try to take us over.

Whether or not they can actually afflict us physiologically (and I believe they can), I'm certainly convinced they afflict us psychologically. There are all kinds of evil spirits. They come in many sizes and shapes. At the lowest rung are what mystics have envisioned as spiritual gnats and fleas. Other mystics have described them as scorpions, because of their sting.

They seem to latch onto our spirits and sting us, chatting all the while, until this bondage is broken.

"For the last few nights I have dreamed that various parts of my body were turning into snakes," wrote the woman in the "three faces of Eve" case. "Each night more of me is consumed by reptiles."

Reptiles. Snakes. Gargoyles. Or scaly hands. There is something within a deceived, oppressed, or possessed person that slithers or tightens like a cobra. No wonder mankind, since time immemorial, has symbolized demons as reptilian. They're cold. They sting. They grasp with immaterial claws. Like a coral snake, or rattler, they're full of venom.

Do demons really look like reptiles?

I don't know. I know only that this is the way they are represented by artists, mystics, and visionaries.

According to one such mystic, a devil once appeared that "looked like part gorilla and part man. The eyes were pure fiery red. The face was like human with strange reactions. It was more human than gorilla, like a combination of man, gorilla, and kangaroo. It moved with a hop.

"On [another] occasion," continued this mystic, "I saw him in a shape like a dog, but with pink eyes and strange feet, with claws, and a face like an alligator. But it talked like a human. There were like three huge black bats falling all over, descending on his back, and one or two more descending on the floor. At one point he promised me anything in his kingdom, which he referred to as earth. Then he would get furious and say he would destroy me—froth and blow it toward where I was and it would burst into flames. I was left shattered to pieces. Then an older woman came and told me to be at peace. I didn't know who it was. She said I wore her symbol around my neck. Then I realized it was Saint Bridget."

Others have seen devils with the face of a grotesque billygoat or in the form of animals like the panther. The panther and similar cats are in their turn similar to the earth spirits that American Indians and Haitian voodooists have long described. Navajos and other Indians believed that stages of the moon brought animal-gods out of the gullies—or at least one particular animal-god which was rather much like a gila monster. When I visited the pyramid fields at Teotihuacan, a place of solstice rituals and pagan blood sacrifice, the panther was greatly in evidence.

In Europe, the werewolf; in China, the dragon.

Look at some of the costumes during the Mardi Gras, or at the closing ceremony of the Barcelona Olympics, or in Broadway plays. Or on Halloween. Saint Teresa of Avila, a doctor of the Church, had many encounters with evil spirits, including one that looked like "a most hideous little [creature], snarling as if in despair at having lost what he was trying to gain... The worst thing had been the interior disquiet: I could find no way of regaining my tranquility."

The Spanish saint was also granted a vision of Hell, and the entrance, she wrote, "resembled a very long, narrow passage, like a furnace, very low, dark and closely confined; the ground seemed to be full of water which looked like filthy, evil-smelling mud, and in it were many wicked-looking reptiles."

This description is like what other mystics have described to me. They have seen hideous images of a place of burbling mud. In that mud are demonic creatures and also condemned, disfigured humans, so ugly because they *hate*. It is presented as a netherworld of smoke and steam. The creatures report to a higher-level demon, presumably on their activities harassing humanity.

That was where the devils came from. That was where condemned humans went. That is what we are fighting. That is what, in prayer, we are victors over.

Saint John Bosco saw the road to Hell as a beautiful and wide path that descended swiftly and suddenly turned into a place with white-hot walls.

Those in deliverance ministry claim the demonic realm has hierarchies and choirs similar to those of Heaven. After all, many demons are fallen angels, and they are counterparts of all that is heavenly—angels, archangels, principalities, powers, virtues, dominations, thrones, cherubim, and seraphim.

How many are there?

We know only that there are many in the hierarchy, for when Satan fell, he took a third of the angels with him, and when Jesus asked the demon possessing the wild man (*Mark* 5:9) what its name was, the demon said, "My name is Legion; for we are many."

There are also condemned humans who, according to some mystics, return to earth seeking to do the living harm.

And along with them all those gnats, bats, and spiritual fleas.

The greatest mystic of our time, Padre Pio of San Giovanni Rotundo, Italy, encountered demons as "wretched creatures" that possessed "the hooves of Lucifer." His spiritual battle, his lifelong struggle with the forces of Satan, was announced to him at the age of 15. In a vision he beheld a majestic man of rare beauty, resplendent as the sun, and this man took him by the hand. *"Come with me, for you must fight a douty warrior,"* he explained, leading Pio to a vast field where there was a great multitude of beings.

The multitude was separated into two groups. On one side were men of terrifically beautiful countenance, clad in radiant white garments, while on the other were men of hideous aspect, dressed in black raiment "like so many dark shadows."

Pio was taken to a place between the two sides when suddenly a terrifying man approached, so tall "his very forehead seemed to touch the heavens, while his face seemed to be that of a Blackamoor, so black and horrible it was."

Pio was told by his angelic guide that he would have to fight this eerie creature, and naturally Pio tried to beg off, arguing with his angel that the man was "so strong that the strength of all men combined could not be sufficient to fell him."

But the angel said he had to fight the fight, and so the young Pio, in spirit, entered into ferocious combat. With the help of his guide he overcame the strongman, throwing him to the ground. The angel rewarded Pio with a crown and said, *"I will reserve for you a crown even more beautiful if you fight the good fight with the being whom you have just fought. He will continually renew the assault to regain his lost honor. Fight valiantly and do not doubt my aid. Keep your eyes wide open, for that mysterious personage will try to take you by surprise. Do not fear his. . . formidable might, but remember what I have promised you: that I will always be close at hand and I will always help you, so that you will always succeed in conquering him.''*

CHAPTER 20

The Truth of the Light

So there are scorpions. There are locusts. There are fallen seraphim and principalities. There are spirits of lust, spirits of obsession, and spirits of anger. There are spirits that have charge of individuals and spirits that beset entire families.

I have found nothing quite so rewarding as the realization that with Christ and the Holy Spirit we have great power over these spirits—that they must flee in the name of Jesus—and that when we cause them to leave, new graces are sent to us from the heavenlies.

In the name of Jesus we rid our environment of the bats and gnats, of the imps that seek to destroy our peace.

Higher up, there are spirits that exercise oppression over neighborhoods, cities, and regions.

Or so we are told by demonologists. I have seen "miraculous" photos taken by charismatics touring Eastern Europe who caught the image of a towering dark figure over a particular town in the late 1980s. It left you with the impression (and only the impression, since such pictures are open to great question) of an upper hierarchical demon whose job it was to coordinate evil in that particular vicinity.

In Indian times curses were placed on tracts of land, especially those that had been used for sacrificial rites, and demonic manifestations have been reported at the sites of "vision quests" or ritual burial.

There are territories. There are strongholds. And the master of principalities, the chief of dominions, is Satan. His power to affect large areas, to hover over a country in the same way angels (such as the Angel of Portugal at Fatima) watch over whole countries, was acknowledged by no less than Pope Paul VI, who saw the devil not only as a "personal spiritual reality," not only a "dark and disturbing spirit," but as a sacred enemy who had been responsible for untold misfortunes in human history.

Perverted and perverting. Highly cunning, beyond our ability to grasp. Mysterious and intimidating. Able to exert his malefic strength upon whole societies.

"The evil which exists in the world is the result and effect of an attack upon us and our society by a dark and hostile agent, the devil," said the Pope during a famous general audience on November 15, 1972. "Evil is not only a privation but a living, spiritual, corrupt and corrupting being. A terrible reality, mysterious and frightening. The testimony of both the Bible and Church tells us that people refuse to acknowledge his existence; or they make of him a self-subsistent principle not originating in God, unlike all creatures; or he is explained away as a pseudo-reality, a fantastic personification of the unknown grounds of the evil within us."

But really, said the Pope, "the devil is the enemy number one, the source of all temptation. Thus we know that this dark and destructive being really exists and is still active; he is the sophistical perverter of man's equilibrium, the malicious seducer who knows how to penetrate us (through the sense, the imagination, desire, utopian logic or disordered social contacts) in order to spread error."

The Pope was concerned because the devil's name had disappeared from the pulpits. It is "very important," said the Pope, "to return to a study of Catholic teaching on the devil and the influence he is able to wield, but nowadays, little attention is paid it."

Instead, Satan is treated as an archetype, a mere image or symbol, the emblem for sin and nothing more. A metaphor. The stuff of Tin Lizzies. When Pope Paul issued his declarations, there was a movement afoot to bid farewell to the very conception of personal evil. "Reformers" and "progressives" didn't like the concept of an interactive devil. It didn't fit within scientific paradigms, and anyway, it was *scary*. They didn't want to "scare" away potential congregants, many of whom were acquiring lifestyles that would fall into unsaintly realms.

Yet that's exactly what the Pope was telling us we were *supposed* to do: discuss the devil, expose his wiles, bring forth the light of truth. For ignoring evil, claiming it's too scary to preach, is what keeps us in darkness.

The truth (*John* 8:32) sets us free.

We are nearly *duty-bound* to do that, said the Pope. It's a clear and present necessity. The devil is infiltrating the Church. Paul VI made that clear on June 29, 1972, when with remarkable candor he fretted "that the smoke of Satan has penetrated the Temple of God through some crack or another."

Satan was perverting the youth, who knew nothing about him. He was confusing the flock. He was blinding the shepherds. He was dangerous the more he was allowed to operate without notice. He was strangling the fruits of Vatican II. He was downgrading the role of Mary, banishing her memoria, and stripping the Church of its majestic aura. He was in the seminaries.

An apostasy was in the making, and so strongly did Pope Paul feel about satanic influence that three years after his "smoke of Satan" remark, the Vatican, through its Congregation for the Doctrine of the Faith, issued a document specifically addressing demonology. Released in June of 1975, the text made clear that if the devil had never been made the object of a dogmatic declaration, this was only because before our modern era it didn't seem *necessary* to expound upon evil force, since its existence is a common assumption integral to "the constant and universal faith of the Church, which is based on its greatest source, namely, the teaching of Christ, and also on that concrete expression of lived faith, the liturgy, which has always insisted on the existence of demons and the threat which they represent."

"Teaching concerning the devil is an undisputed element

of the Christian awareness,'' added the document, while Pope Paul, a year before he died, returned to the same theme in yet another exhortation: "It is no wonder if our society is disintegrating when Holy Scripture sharply warns us that 'the whole world (in a pejorative sense) is under the power of the evil one' who is also called 'the prince of this world.'''

The Pope was sensing something the rest of the world did not care to appreciate. His remarks created an uproar. News commentators lambasted him. Modernists ignored him. Humanists laughed. The devil! Superstition! Swayed by secular forces, priests maintained a disturbing, almost conspiratorial silence, while in many Protestant circles the focus shifted toward prosperity ministry, which carried disturbing parallels to the New Age and human-potential movements sweeping America.

The modernists were at high dudgeon. They began broaching the possibility that Jesus wasn't infallible, that He may not have known He was Messianic, that He did not institute the Church, and that His Resurrection—long a sore point with scientists who disdained *all* miracles— was not a fact of the historical order.

It was enough for people to try to comprehend God, in other words, without Satan and all the other mysticism.

Which was just fine with the devil, that Christians as well as Jews were questioning their religious precepts, some making a dirty word out of "fundamentalism."

Tenets that had stood for more than 1,900 years, and that in some instances went back to Moses or even the Garden, were now subject to great and searing question. This was especially true in liberal factions of American Protestantism. A full decade before Pope Paul's remarks a survey conducted by *Redbook* magazine claimed to show that 56 percent of ministers in training rejected the virgin birth of Jesus; 54 percent rejected the bodily resurrection; and 71 percent even doubted there was life after death.

Warnings that sin would lead to Hell, or to earthly tribulation, as at Sodom and Gomorrah, were ridiculed as "doom-and-gloom"; if the Church was to survive in an age of materialistic liberalism it was going to have to learn leniency and a *positive* attitude, like the "positive" attitudes they were teaching at Esalen, like what they were teaching with transcendental meditation.

Aummm-oooommmmm.

The Church was going to have to compromise, get a little *New Agey.*

It was going to have to get with it if it wanted to be accepted into the latter part of the twentieth century.

Especially, most especially, it was going to have to stop any blather about Satan and demons.

Who could really lay all the blame on the poor priests? They were in a cultural maelstrom. They were in a culture of lawyers and scientists, a culture where faith had been butted aside by scientism and legalism. As Mary had warned a century before, during her apparition in 1846 at LaSalette, demons were being loosed from Hell to put an end to faith *"little by little."* They were blinding men in such a way that humans would take on the spirit of demons themselves—a spirit of anti-christ. Our Blessed Mother had warned that several religious institutions would lose faith altogether, a prophecy that was at least partly fulfilled in New York, where 346 priests, 1,730 sisters, and 531 seminarians would be lost between 1970 and 1990 in the Brooklyn diocese alone, while nations like Holland and France saw regular church attendance drop to around 10 percent.

Poor priests. Poor rabbis and ministers. They stood as the last vestiges of spiritual nobility. It was no wonder that many of them grew to question their faith or fell into scandal.

In the age of science, with biologists now able to define DNA and send probes to the outer reaches of the solar system, with no sign yet of angels, was there really much room for a *spirit* world?

And wasn't it true that many of the things once attributed to the forces of the supernatural—rain, lightning—were now explicable through simple meteorology?

A material society accepted only that which could be measured or photographed, and no one had pictures of the Holy Spirit.

Add to this the scandals. Ministers and priests were the subject of burgeoning scandals, scandals that were exagger-

ated by the press, scandals that were to a lesser degree than
those readily found in other American professions, including journalism, scandals that were often blown out of
proportion considering that there were 51,000 priests in the
U.S., the majority good, but scandals nonetheless, in fulfillment of another LaSalette prophecy:

*"The priests, the ministers of my Son, the priests, by their
wicked lives, by their irreverence and their impiety in the
celebration of the Holy Mysteries, by their love of money,
their love of honors and pleasures, the priests have become
cesspools of impurity. Yes, the priests are asking for vengeance, and vengeance is hanging over their heads. Woe
to priests and to those dedicated to God who by their infi-
delity and their wicked lives are crucifying my Son again."*

While the Catholic Church managed to maintain and
even add to its formal membership (those who may not be
going to church on Sunday but at least *call* themselves
Catholics), mainline Judaism and Protestantism saw their
numbers decrease precipitously. Nearly half the children
born as Presbyterians, Methodists, or Episcopalians would
end up leaving those denominations permanently, and six
major Protestant denominations reported a combined net
membership loss of 6.2 million between the mid-1960s and
1992. Gone were a *third* of the Presbyterians.

Those who remained in the pews heard sermons and
homilies that, devoid of mysticism, had become dry philosophy. Where was the Holy Spirit? Where was denunciation
of great and rising evils such as abortion, adultery, and
homosexuality?

The priests had grown battle-weary, disparaged on *60
Minutes,* deplored at the movies, ridiculed on *Saturday
Night Live.* If the smoke of Satan had entered the Church,
the fires had been lit by spiritless theologians and the
increasingly sardonic media.

Newspapers, television, and Hollywood, which considered it such a relic, weren't going to leave the Church alone
until they had scared every last deacon out of the seminary.

Scared them or *enticed* them out. Everywhere they
turned, priests felt left out, their exquisite sacrifice of
celibacy, which enriched them with Spirit, grossly
misunderstood—made to feel like eunuchs. Didn't they

know, asked the press, that this was the age of liberation? Didn't they know that everyone was doing it? Didn't they know that lust was the fulfillment of humanity?

Didn't they know that, married or unmarried, 95.4 percent of men had sexual relations (see the Guttmacher Institute), and that a quarter of them could list at least twenty sex partners?

Come on and enjoy the fun, said the press, have a scandal—and then we'll go and splash your mugs on *60 Minutes.*

When priests looked for comfort to Rome they saw a heroic Pope but one who, betrayed by the hierarchy, was surrounded with financial embarrassments. There had even been questions—very serious questions—about the international dealings of the Vatican Bank, which bore unsavory connections to Sicilian bank swindler Michele Sindona as well as Licio Gelli, grand master of Masonic Lodge P2 and one of the most powerful Masons in the world. Speculation still abounds at how Pope John Paul I, who sought to purge the Vatican of its questionable banking procedures, met his untimely death after only 33 days on the throne of Peter.

"Woe to the Princes of the Church whose only occupation will be to heap wealth upon more wealth, and to preserve their authority and proud domination!" said the Virgin of LaSalette. *"The Vicar of my Son will have much to suffer, and, for a time, the Church will yield to large persecution, a time of darkness, and the Church will suffer a frightful crisis. As the holy faith of God is forgotten, every individual will wish to be his own guide and be superior to his fellow men. Civil and ecclesiastical authority will be abolished. All order and justice will be trampled underfoot. Nothing will be seen but murder, hatred, jealousy, falsehood, and the discord without love for the mother country or for the family."*

All the secular powers would have one and the same plan, warned the Virgin of LaSalette, and that would be *"to abolish and do away with every religious principle, to make way for materialism, atheism, spiritualism, and vice of all kinds."*

CHAPTER 21

The Secrets of LaSalette and Fatima

This same set of affairs, the crisis within formal Christendom, was indicated at Fatima, where the youngest of the three visionaries, Jacinta Marto, a mere seven-year-old when Mary appeared in 1917, had been granted a vision in which she saw the Pope kneeling by a table in a very big house, his head buried in his hands, weeping, many people outside, cursing and throwing stones.

The faith was in jeopardy. That was at least part of the secret told the Fatima children. A portion of the spiritual chastisement was already underway. More was to come. It was contained in the third part of the messages the older girl, Lucia dos Santos, had been given by the Virgin on July 13, 1917. The first two parts of the secret involved the vision of Hell along with a prediction that World War I would soon end but a greater war would erupt if mankind did not repent and institute a devotion known as the Communion of Reparation on the first Saturday of each month. The onset of that predicted war was to be announced by *"a night illuminated by an unknown light,"* which materialized as a magnificent display in the sky of what scientists claimed was an extremely unusual aurora borealis or "northern lights" on January 25, 1938—a month before

Hitler marched into Austria, seeking just that war. Mary also said in 1917 that if Russia was not converted and consecrated to her Immaculate Heart, that huge nation would *"spread her errors throughout the world, causing wars and persecutions of the Church."* This was told to these little peasant children in 1917, four months before the Bolsheviks overthrew the Russian czar, paving the way for Communism.

Hellfire and rumors of war filled the first two parts of Our Lady's message, while a last part, the Third Secret, has never been released publicly. Only three living people are known to be familiar with its contents: Lucia, the Pope, and Joseph Cardinal Ratzinger. We know only that it begins with these telling words: *"In Portugal, the dogma of the Faith will always be preserved. . ."*

Faith. It has to do with faith. A crisis in the Church. A crisis that would affect many nations, but not so much Portugal. As Father Joaquin Maria Alonso, who prepared the definitive study of Fatima, points out, if in Portugal the dogma of the Faith will always be preserved, "it can be clearly deduced from this that in other parts of the Church these dogmas are going to become obscure or even lost altogether. It is quite possible that the message not only speaks of a 'crisis of faith' in the Church during this period, but also, like the secrets of LaSalette, that it makes concrete references to internal strife among Catholics and to the deficiencies of priests and the religious. It is also possible that it may imply deficiencies even among the upper ranks of the hierarchy."

Indeed, at LaSalette, in 1846, Mary had forecast *"a time of darkness"* during which *"the Church will witness a frightful crisis,"* warning that *"the devil will resort to all his evil tricks to introduce sinners into religious orders, for disorder and the love of carnal pleasures will be spread all over the earth."* There would be attempts to harm the Holy Father, said LaSalette, and *"a great number of priests and members of religious orders will break away from the true religion; among these people there will be even bishops."* Churches, she said, would be *"locked up or desecrated"* while others would be built to serve *"spirits of darkness."* A "forerunner" of the Anti-Christ would arrive to fight against the True Christ, followed, at some unknown juncture in the near or distant future, by the Anti-Christ himself.

No doubt: LaSalette had been very concerned with the state of Christianity, and so was the Third Secret of Fatima. Such was further indicated by remarks Pope Paul VI made on May 13, 1967, when, having read the secret, he traveled to Fatima for the fiftieth anniversary of the first apparition and seemed preoccupied with Church affairs, especially maintaining "a united Church, a holy Church." Terrible damage could be provoked, he warned, "by arbitrary interpretations, not authorized by the teaching of the Church, disrupting its traditional and constitutional structure, replacing the theology of the true and great Fathers of the Church with new and peculiar theologies; interpretations intent upon stripping the norms of faith of that which modern thought, often lacking rational judgment, does not understand and does not like. Such interpretations change the apostolic fervor of redeeming charity to the negative structures of a profane mentality and of worldly customs."

In other words, Paul VI was fretting about modernism and the misapplication of Vatican II. Modernism was what one of his predecessors, the great Pius X, had called "the synthesis of all heresies." And it would soon wend its way through most denominations of Christianity, arrogating man to godhead, excusing serious sin, looking the other way from sacrilege, tolerating promiscuity as a simple transgression, remaining quiet over abortion, dismissing notions of the devil, ignoring deliverance as a ministry, demoting Mary, treating the New Testament more as a parable than a historical document, edging away from belief in Christ's miracles, and most blatantly of all, replacing spirituality with cold hard philosophy. In Catholicism it would be most readily seen in de-emphasis of Confession, downgrading of the Rosary and Blessed Sacrament (in some cases tabernacles were removed to another room), laxity in handing out annulments (which were penned now by the truckload), informality and lack of serious instruction during Mass, and the removal of noble sacramentals, especially crucifixes and statues of the Virgin, who was so often portrayed stepping on the head of the serpent, which the devil could not have liked one bit.

In short, bingo had replaced Holy Hour.

Many of these trends were the result of simple and understandable fear, especially the fear that Church discipline, in the face of an increasingly undisciplined culture, would chase yet more from the pews. Who would be left, if every other young person who wanted to remarry after a failed first marriage was faced with rebuke? Thanks to the culture, marriage was now founded largely upon sexuality instead of spiritual love, and this diluted the moxie with which young people were bound. When the sex got old the bricks fell into rubble. Meanwhile, Protestants and Catholics were seeing many of their young defecting to new congregations founded by anyone who had a microphone and a New Testament. That Tammy Bakker and Jimmy Swaggart could be major figures in American Christianity told the story in a nutshell.

The devil's plan was to vomit a deluge (*Revelation* 12:15) so as to sweep away the Virgin, and the flood of his water contained two key ingredients: the poison of those who declared Mary an idol, saying there was nothing to substantiate her veneration in the Bible; and, at the other extremity, false claims—diluting claims—of the many, the deceived many, who said they heard her voice but really did not.

No wonder Billy Graham and the Fatima scholars saw everything coming apart. In 1984, at a place called Akita, Japan, the local ordinary, Bishop John Shojiro Ito, issued a pastoral letter authorizing veneration of a miracle which had occurred to a nun named Sister Agnes Katsuko Sasagawa, who said the Virgin had told her *"the work of the devil will infiltrate even into the Church in such a way that one will see cardinals opposing cardinals, bishops against other bishops. The priests who venerate me will be scorned and opposed by their confreres. . .churches and altars will be sacked; the Church will be full of those who accept compromises and the demon will press many priests and consecrated souls to leave the service of the Lord. The demon will be especially implacable against souls consecrated to God."*

Mary also told Sister Agnes that if mankind continued

to allow Satan to thrive in its midst, God was going to *"inflict a terrible punishment on all humanity."* According to Joseph Cardinal Ratzinger, who approved the pastoral letter, Akita's message is essentially the same as Fatima's Third Secret. This he implied during the summer of 1990 to Howard Q. Dee, ambassador from the Philippines to the Vatican. In an interview with journalist Vittorio Messori, Ratzinger, the second most powerful man in Catholicism, prodded on it further, telling Messori the Third Secret involves "a radical call to conversion, the absolute seriousness of history, the dangers threatening the faith and life of the Christian, and therefore the world. And also the importance of the Last Times." The things contained in the Third Secret correspond, according to Ratzinger, "to what is announced in Scripture and are confirmed by many other Marian apparitions, beginning with the Fatima apparitions themselves in their known content."

Were not the signs at apparitional sites, the *authentic* sites, from Venezuela to the Middle East—the signs in the sky and the flashes of light—pertinent to *Revelation* 11:19?

There was the hint that Fatima's great secret might therefore involve more than just Church matters and may have something to say about an actual worldly chastisement or eschatological punishment. Such was certainly the case at LaSalette, which was just full of prophecies that had already materialized in the most impressive format. As the Virgin predicted to Melanie Calvat in 1846, Satan had bedimmed the intelligence of our leaders and caused the massive break-up of families, although no one could have foreseen a divorce rate of around fifty percent for young people by the 1990s; she said *"voices will be heard in the air,"* and indeed there was a flurry of spirit channeling, as well as the false locutions; and she said people would grow cold and secular, though few were the indications that one day it would be looked upon as sociopathic to recite a prayer in school while the killing of preborn humans, on the other hand, would become a right under formal jurisprudence. *"Physical and moral agonies will be suffered,"* Mary had said. *"God will abandon mankind to itself."*

There would thus be more than moral agonies. There would also be *physical* ones: famines, plagues, wars. She said there would be earthquakes and frightful new storms as nature asked for *"vengeance."*

The earth, said Mary, *"will be struck by calamities of all kinds (in addition to plague and famine which will be widespread),"* and she alluded to infectious disease.

"The seasons will be altered," she said, and I wondered if it was true what scientists were telling me several years ago as I embarked upon a new environmental book for Harper & Row: that "greenhouse gases" and molecules of chlorine were causing "global warming" and a hole in the ozone layer, which shields us from cancer-causing ultraviolet radiation.

I don't know if the climate has yet actually been affected, nor do the scientists, but working on that book *(The Toxic Cloud),* I knew there were growing environmental perils.

So too were there other trends, such as the spreading epidemic of stress and hypertension—of heart attacks—which indicated that some form of chastisement was already in subtle progress.

In modern America, in scientific America, in plasticized America, one in every four or five people was contracting cancer, some of it from the pollution of food and waterways (witches have long been known to use poison in their rituals).

"The prince of evil pours out his venom today with all his might, because he sees his sorry reign is ending and little is left to him," said Mary at another locally approved site in Argentina. (I have tried, with the exception of Medjugorje, to stick only with those apparitional cases approved by the local bishop of the Church.)

Mary urged reconciliation of all nations and faiths in face of growing evils which eventually would graduate to an eruption of some sort, an event that finally would make the front page. More important than any physical punishment, however, was the spiritual chastisement, orchestrated by the furies who sowed dissension within the Church and were oppressing the general population in a way that cried out for deliverance. They were trying to drag as many as possible down to the fire and mud. As Sister

Lucia of Fatima explained, the mission was not to indicate to the world *material* or physical punishments (which, nonetheless, she said seemed certain to come), but "to indicate to everyone the imminent danger we are in of losing our souls for all eternity if we remain obstinate in sin.

"Our Lady did not tell me that we are living in the last epoch of the world, but she did give me to understand that, firstly, we are going through a decisive battle, at the end of which we will be either of God or of the Evil One: there will be no middle way; secondly, that the last means God will give to the world for its salvation are the Holy Rosary and the devotion to the Immaculate Heart; and thirdly, when God, in His Providence, is about to chastise the world, He first uses every means to save us, and when He sees we have not made use of them, then He gives us the last anchor of salvation, His mother."

Sister Lucia emphasized that "the devil is carrying on a decisive battle with the Virgin Mary. He sees that his time is getting short, and he is making every effort to gain as many souls as possible. He wants to get hold of consecrated souls."

No question: God had put enmity *(Genesis* 3:15) between the serpent and the sun-clad woman *(Revelation* 12:1).

Sister Lucia herself said the Third Secret is in the Book of Revelation, and *Revelation,* so well recognized by Pius X and Paul VI, makes reference to Satan as the "seducer of the whole world." No one knew how long it would last, but the final battle was beginning, the battle, said Sister Lucia, "where one side will be victorious and the other side will suffer defeat. Hence from now on we must choose sides. Either we are for God, or we are for the devil. There is no other possibility."

"Is God less powerful than the devil?" asked the Fatima seer. "It is necessary to go forward without fear and without trepidation. God is with us, and He will be victorious."

She further explained that the devil "knows that religious and priests who fall away from their beautiful vocation drag numerous souls to Hell," and so he "wishes to take possession of consecrated souls. He tries to corrupt them in order to lull to sleep the souls of lay people and thereby lead them to final impenitence. He employs all tricks, even going so far as to suggest the delay of entrance into religious life. Resulting from this is the sterility of the interior life, and among the lay people, coldness (lack of enthusiasm) regarding the subject of renouncing pleasures and the total dedication of themselves to God.''

So too had the Virgin of LaSalette called upon *"the apostles of the last days, the faithful disciples of Jesus Christ who have lived in scorn for the world and for themselves, in poverty and in humility, in scorn and in silence, in prayer and mortification, in chastity and in union with God, in suffering and unknown to the world. It is time they came out and filled the world with light. Go and reveal yourselves to be my cherished children...*

"Fight, children of light, you, the few who can see..."

CHAPTER 22

The Doctrine of Devils

It was John Paul II himself who on May 13, 1982, the Fatima feast day, spoke of himself as "a witness to the almost apocalyptic menaces looking over the nations and mankind as a whole."

It was no exaggeration. This was true spiritual war. This was true manifestation of evil seraphim, cherubim, powers, and principalities. I wasn't superstitious, but when I visited LaSalette, high in the French Alps, it was snowing as I got out of my car, but at that very moment there was a resounding clap of thunder.

Ah, yes: war. War was in the wind. Lucifer was rising. There was the echo of distant but approaching thunder. The devil had been released (*Revelation* 20:1-9) from the pit, and now was free to roam as the Great Seducer, tempter par excellence, the Deceiver.

Dangerous times. The personal suffering was increasing, the moral suffering was miserable, and in New York, the AIDS epidemic—*infectious disease*—was such that at rush hour you could expect at least one or two people in every car of the subway to be carrying the HIV virus.

The virus, I must add, has never been cured.

At the same time AIDS demonstrated the limits of medicine, the horrible explosion of the space shuttle testified to the limits of man's other technological powers.

140

Most frightful, and most suppressed, was the epidemic of satanic-ritual abuse, so prevalent today that a 1991 survey of members of the American Psychological Association found that thirty percent—a third—of respondents had encountered one or more clients said to have suffered from just such ritualism.

Mary was forecasting a set of spiritual afflictions or chastisements that would develop gradually and cause a great oppression. Family troubles and personal ailments would coincide with godlessness, disorientation, and societal unrest. Demons would strike at will, and we would encounter nothing but the filth of Hell the longer we wallowed in disobedience.

These agonies would in their turn evolve into seemingly disconnected famines and wars, little wars at first, little indications from nature at first, but over the years, over the decades, building into larger and larger punishments—chastisements fashioned by human hands, as God *"abandoned mankind to itself."*

No one would be able to escape so many afflictions together.

Gradually, God's Justice was coming into play, and He was nudging us to break the evil. He wanted us to prove ourselves by fighting valiantly, fighting without ceasing, fighting to the bitter end against the forces of darkness.

It was equally obvious that the Lord had chosen the Virgin to collect a little army of noble souls to break the might and bondages of Lucifer through prayer and sacrifice. Only if the devil's strongholds were broken would mankind avert the sort of difficulties, even disasters, otherwise looming in the uncharted future.

We need to learn from the Angel of Portugal, who, upon his third visit to Fatima, held aloft a chalice with the Host suspended above and leaving it suspended in mid-air prostrated himself and repeated a prayer essential to lessening whatever events may await us: *"Most Holy Trinity, Father, Son, and Holy Spirit, I adore You profoundly and I offer You the most precious Body, Blood, Soul, and Divinity of Jesus Christ, present in all the tabernacles of the world, in reparation for the outrages, sacrileges, and indifference by which He is offended. And by the infinite merits of His Most*

Sacred Heart and the Immaculate Heart of Mary, I beg of You the conversion of poor sinners."

The angel had then given the Host to Lucia and the contents of the chalice to Jacinta and Francisco, saying, *"Take and drink the Body and Blood of Jesus Christ, horribly outraged by ungrateful men. Make reparation for their crimes and console your God."*

Otherwise the pews would continue to tremble. Otherwise more souls would head into darkness. It is absolutely imperative to convert sinners or we will all be held to account. The more souls that are lost, said Mary, the closer man comes to major chastisement. "Her plan is to give constant battle to demons," wrote one exorcist, "to wrest a large number of souls from them and to cast the helpless demons back into Hell."

I didn't care what my colleagues in journalism believed, I *saw* manifestations of evil, in some cases supernatural signs. I saw it when I was working on an article about pollution of the Mississippi River for *Science Digest*. Up there at Lake Itasca, at the river's headwaters, surveying the sky during a violent thunderstorm, which had caused a greenish tint, indicating tornadoes, the clouds roiled into a formation resembling a huge and perfect skull.

Spiritual war was in the wind, alright, almost total warfare. It was the age of the false prophet—not just the imams of Iran or the yogis from India, not just instructors of esp, but false prophets and Dr. Feelgoods who were leading souls astray within the domain of Christianity; ravening wolves, in sheep's clothing.

Pius X, pontiff at the onset of the century, had seen it coming. He had called it a "universal flood of errors." He had seen that the "reformers" were fomenting "a universal denial of the Church's faith and discipline."

It was an apostasy more disastrous than the one which had darkened the century Saint Charles lived in.

It was a poison, said Pius, that slips "artfully and mysteriously" into the Church's "very blood vessels."

"It is the spirit of lies and perfidiousness, hidden," said Pius, "under the veils of Catholicism, which undertook to place religion at the service of the enemies' power."

Was modernism the false prophet of *Revelation?*

The same satanic rage that had decimated the cultures of Russia and China, had enslaved about half of the world, had led to at least 100 million dead at the hands of the "red dragon," was now in the West, working more subtly but with ferocious tenacity. It was an ingenious spirit, moving easily in a technological culture, seeking above all to make religion appear unscientific and thus not only out of step but intellectually minuscule.

From the Sixties through the Nineties the battle would heat up, much of it fought within the Church, much of it to do with other books of the Bible like *Jude* (17-19), which warned that "in the last days there will be imposters living by their godless passions. These sensualists, devoid of the Spirit, are causing divisions among you."

Paul the Apostle had issued similar warnings, especially in his epistles to Titus and Timothy. "The Spirit distinctly says that in later times some will turn away from the faith and will heed deceitful spirits and things taught by demons through plausible liars. . . (*1 Timothy* 4:1-2)."

The King James Version calls it the "doctrine of demons."

Men, warned Paul, would become "lovers of self and of money, proud, arrogant, abusive, disobedient to their parents, ungrateful, profane, inhuman, implacable, slanderous, licentious, brutal, hating the good. They will be treacherous, reckless, pompous, lovers of pleasure rather than of God as they make a pretense of religion but negate its power. (*2 Timothy* 3:2-5)."

Could anyone offer a better critique of modern culture?

"Modern times are dominated by Satan and will be more so in the future," added Saint Maximilian Kolbe. "The conflict with Hell cannot be engaged in by men, even the most clever. The Immaculata alone has from God the promise of victory over Satan."

It was a war, in other words, that had to be fought through prayer in the realm of the supernatural. It had to be fought in the name of Christ through the Holy Spirit with the help of Mary. It was a war, again, in the heavenlies. Pius X had prophesied that the time was at hand when society would attempt to uproot and destroy "all relations between man and the Divinity."

Devils would transform themselves, Paul had warned (*2 Corinthians* 11:15), into "ministers of righteousness."

We were now seeing that. We were seeing the devil as an angel of light. We were seeing ministers of righteousness—calling themselves humanists—teaching at our schools and sitting on our courts. The doctrine of liberalism. The doctrine of easy penance. The doctrine of readily excusing sin in the name of kindness and humanism.

It's okay, Johnny. It's okay.

The doctrine of demons. Who could really doubt it? The rebellious spirit of the Sixties had inserted itself into the mainstream of the Seventies, Eighties, and Nineties. There was no more need to wear worn-out jeans and shout on the streets. Rebellion had been *institutionalized*. What once had been the province of criminals or radicals was now permeating the mainstream. Drug use had spread from college to the local junior high, and in some cases even into elementary grades.

Now residents of once-quiet suburban towns needed not just dead-bolts but cans of Mace, a hefty dog, and an alarm system.

That was a true chastisement: the increase in crime. Woe to a society that had seen four million crimes in 1960 but now 15 million a year by 1990.

In three decades crimes of violence increased 500 percent and there was a *tripling* of teenage suicides.

Who needed tidal waves? Society was its own apocalypse. Feminism stripped away the traditional role of motherhood—made it seem like something unproductive—and with teens fornication, once the province only of the neighborhood Jezebel, had replaced necking.

The spirit of Jezebel was on the rise as handmaid to Lucifer.

And when sexual lust dominates a society, a lust for blood is often close behind. Whips and chains showed up in the girlie magazines and then on cable television. Soon the poison of sado-masochism graduated into a remarkable array of serial killers who, unwatched by a liberal system of justice, went so far as necrophilia and cannibalism.

By the mid-1970s, when the Vatican issued its dissertation on demonism, there were fewer hippies and long-haired rock concerts, but that's because they no longer felt the need to openly promote their moral agenda: the radicalism of the Sixties had become the rule of the day. Hippies hadn't disappeared. They had simply put on suits and ties, or were in Hollywood writing screenplays.

Taking the reins from Hefner, these "artists" brought the Playboy "philosophy" into every home and made it available to all of our children.

The sex-liberators and agnostics in Studio City, or on their beach decks in Malibu, were the new Aristotles.

Could even the Apostle Paul have foreseen such treachery?

When asked about the sex and violence in movies, director Oliver Stone (of *Wall Street* and *JFK* fame), ridiculed the "age-old" fear that movies had become satanic. He didn't see any moral boundaries. "You can do anything as long as you do it well," he told *The New Yorker*. "I think Hitler would make a great movie."

At Disney, Chairman Michael Eisner said that while his own studio stayed away from violent films, he agonizes little over morality. "It's not a moral issue," he said of those who do make violent films. "I'm glad they do it. It brings people to the movie theatre."

Disney! There were more than 3,000 studies showing that TV affects the attitude and behavior of viewers, but that didn't concern Hollywood, which kept cranking out mass-market records, videos, and films in which, as critic Michael Medved pointed out, performers drink urine, rip out toenails (with pliers), and torture females.

In his 1991 video "Black or White," singer Michael Jackson—an idol of the young—grabbed a trash container and heaved it through a store window. He also grabbed his crotch and simulated masturbation not once, but a dozen of times.

Marriage was okay, but you really didn't have to get married and if you did, you didn't have to have a family.

The Cleavers were *yesterday.*

Few were the newlyweds who wanted children right off the bat. The "Me Generation" meant just that; children were not to get in the way of career advancement and the pleasures of a new and carnal relationship.

It all came *dangerously* close to the old dictum of Aleister "The Beast" Crowley: "Do what thou wilt shall be the whole of the law."

Was it extreme to suggest that Western culture was heading in a collective way toward institutionalizing not just rebellion but the very craftsmanship of paganism and satanism? Leftists continued to chip away at institutions that represented the stodgy old "establishment" and found ways of defending any type of outrageous behavior under the pretext of "human rights." While most often he cloaked his presence, there were times, especially in the music trade, when the devil became so bold as to show his actual face. No longer did he hide in clever lyrics or backward masking. One band called AC/DC sprouted horns on a 1979 album called *Highway to Hell*, and bassist Gene Simmons of the band Kiss spat blood and breathed fire, mimicking the classic descriptions of demonology.

Another group, Iron Maiden, came out with an album called *The Number of the Beast*. Yet a third had a song called "Possessed."

To look at an album cover was to peer into a coven. There were bands called the Scorpions, Black Sabbath, Suicidal Tendencies, and Judas Priest. Some wore masks that turned them fully demonic, or wore leather, chains, and studs, the paraphernalia of sado-masochism. With or without cosmetics, their long ghoulish looks, their drug-sunken cheeks, and their hardened eyes qualified them for anyone's worst nightmare.

CHAPTER 23

The Demon of Magic

They can't win. The bad spirits won't win. We were told at Fatima that in the end, Mary's Immaculate Heart, making the way for the reign of the Sacred Heart of Jesus, would be victorious. But to bring about that victory before matters become so evil that God will have to forcefully intervene, we must begin by cleaning our own spiritual households, praying to the Spirit for deliverance.

Purge us, oh Lord. Purge us, oh Holy Spirit. Purge us in the name of Jesus, by His all-powerful blood, of any demon, any spirit, any evil entity which may afflict us. Break all our bondages! Purge evil from all our generations! Lead us to deliverance! Let us always listen closely to our spiritual elders. Lead us to the proper guidance of priests and ministers. Illuminate our way. Let us not become obsessed with evil or devils. Let us not be fearful or discouraged. Let us not imagine them where they are not, nor give them credit they do not deserve. But let us know the enemy, the masks he wears, and let us retain what information is useful to our spiritual growth. Lead us to self-control and courage. Deliver us, oh Lord, and send us out, filled with your power, under guidance of Your Spirit and Church, to move forward in prayer, never stepping too fast, but moving forward to break through the strongholds that enslave our poor world, especially the strongholds of sensuality and occultism.

Whether it be heavy metal or the use of drugs, much of our social evil has roots in occultism, or what Our Lady of LaSalette called *"the demon of magic."*
Today we call it New Age.
Back when I was investigating psychic phenomena, if you remember, I thought I was onto something new, an undiscovered mental power. But it's not mental power, it's *spiritual* power, and when it doesn't come through the Holy Spirit and Christ, it's coming from the dark side. When it is not of God, we're tapping into demonic forces that grant us certain supernormal perceptions, alright, but at an exorbitant price. In so doing we invite them into our souls.
They say it's "New Age" but really it's the Old Age in a new bottle. As the years went on I saw that what I had at first believed to be an undiscovered "energy" was actually an occult force that went back to the Neanderthals. Right from cavemen times to the present, humans have been using various means to invoke good luck or supernatural forces (cavemen placed a mutilated skull in a ring of stones), and it was most evident in ancient Egyptian paganism, Babylonian temple worship, the Druid ceremonies at Stonehenge, African voodoo, secret cults like the Knights Templars and Masons, or plain old wizards and witches in Europe.
Great "thinkers" like Alfred Wallace, co-founder with Charles Darwin of evolution's natural-selection theory, were reportedly adherents of spiritualistic phenomena in one form or another. So was a founder of modern psychology, Carl Jung, who developed his theories with the aid of a spirit "guide" named Philemon.

Occultism has survived the ages in hundreds of forms. We've all been touched by it. It comes through astrology, numerology, crystals, pyramid power, channeling, fortunetelling, Taoism, Eastern meditation, superstitions, visualization, occult books, charms, amulets, pagan images, hypnosis, C'hi (or "Ki"), psychokinesis, psychic healing, automatic writing, false locutions, mantras, palm reading, witchcraft (both "black" and "white"), precognition, Santeria, Tarot cards, Atlantis, reincarnation, yoga, "inner space," self-actualization, "higher self," biofeedback, dianetics, global consciousness, color therapy, mind travel, New Age music, transpersonal psychology, water divination, tea-leaf readers, crystal balls, pendulums, rainbows, centaurs, unicorns, ying-yang, enneagram, UFOs, Mother Earth, occult symbols like the anhk, the horn of the "evil-eye," the five-pointed star, the all-seeing eye, or the swastika, and through anything else that smacks of paganism, mediumship or parapsychology.

It's everywhere from the workplace to our schools. According to *The New York Times,* many major corporations have had New Agers give seminars for their executives, and there are 1,000 channellers—people allowing spirits to speak through their voices—in the Los Angeles area alone. I have heard accounts of a priest in the Midwest who hands out crystals (the quartz or other rocks supposed to bring the right energy forces) and meditates at a New Age power spot. He also takes parishioners to a Tarot reader.

So widespread are New Age beliefs that they have influenced otherwise model Christians, and have infiltrated convents, as well as the National Catholic Education Association, which has had New Ager Robert Muller as keynoter at its annual convention. Muller's ideas can be found in writings published by Lucis Trust, an esoteric organization based on the teachings of occultist Madame Blavatsky and once known, until they thought it better to soften the name, as "Lucifer Publishing." These and other peculiarities can be found in three books I must recommend to you, *The Unicorn in the Sanctuary* (by Randy England), *Ungodly Rage* (by Donna Steichen), and *The Hidden Dangers of the Rainbow* (by Constance Cumbey). Back when I was a reporter I wrote a story about a Catholic school in Binghamton, New York, that was teaching its children Silva Mind Control.

A unicorn in the sanctuary. Satan as an angel of light. Satan as self-help guru, telling us that we can all be gods, when really it's what *Deuteronomy* (18:12) calls an "abomination." That the occult is manifesting to such an extent, in so many forms, was an indication to me that our culture is truly on the wrong road—and that the genie is out of the bottle. We had entered serious times. Hell was suddenly everywhere. It was indeed what Sister Lucia had called the "decisive battle." In New York you can pick up a weekly newspaper, the *Village Voice*, and find ads for New Age shops, ritual stores, and theatres presenting plays about sado-masochism. There is phone sex, escort services. There are lawyers advertising divorces for $495 while doctors set the price of an abortion at $195 and accept credit cards like the callgirls.

I'd seen an article on Medjugorje but had no idea that Mary was warning visionaries there, as well as elsewhere, of the seriousness of our times and the darkening clouds. *"Pray, pray, pray,"* she said. *"Do not be discouraged. Be in peace because God gives you the Grace to defeat Satan."*

I kept to the Rosary but also began praying with non-denominational charismatics on the Lower East Side in the heart of Manhattan's debauchery. We prayed with homeless people, who were delivered of demons; we prayed with homosexuals who turned straight; we prayed in tongues and over again said, "Jesus, Jesus, Jesus," feeling the promised grace, knowing that the world's situation wasn't looking good but that one day the war would be won.

We prayed for deliverance from occult spirits, and felt them leave. We broke sexual and New Age bondages. We came against the hovering principalities, and we bound evil spirits. We prayed over people whose involvement with the occult had caused great turmoil in their lives, and in some cases emotional and psychological disorders. We prayed for homosexuals, who are often plagued by feminine spirits or a spirit of witchcraft, and we prayed for those who'd had abortions, for this causes tremendous spiritual bondage, worse even than the occult. We attended seminars on spiritual warfare and learned how demons grip onto us and invade our being, leaving only by the Blood of Christ. I saw a young man who had been homeless, living on the sidewalks, transformed almost overnight into a clean-shaven and respectable churchgoer who couldn't stop praising Jesus.

That's what it's all about: praising, praising, praising.

When we take special time out to thank Heaven, when we thank Jesus by name, over and over, evil oppression is lifted and the way is paved for the Spirit. *Thank you, Jesus. Thank you, Jesus. Thank you, Jesus.*

By instinct I began to fast whole days taking only a few glasses of water. There is nothing like fasting to break spiritual bondages and cast away unpleasant spirits. Jesus clued us in on that. He told us how powerful fasting is in deliverance when His disciples had problems casting the demon out of an epileptic (*Matthew* 17:21). He explained that they had failed due to lack of faith and because *"this kind does not go out except by prayer and fasting."*

So too, does an open Bible set in the middle of a room, especially to *Psalm* 23, discourage foul spirits.

The Lord rebuke you, Satan! The Lord rebuke your occultism!

It is so dangerous, sorcery, especially the Ouija board, which is like calling out for any spirit to enter your home. I saw a case where people using a Ouija board in a haunted house watched the words "I will kill Jimmy" spell out. It referred to a boy living downstairs. The next day, to their horror, Jimmy's parents caught his brother chasing him with a shotgun that had been hidden behind a pile of firewood yet somehow had found itself in the open and was grabbed by the youngster. One of the participants in the Ouija seance began hearing a voice in his head and nearly suffered a nervous breakdown.

The Ouija board conjures up spirits which can cause emotional distress, sexual deviance, involvement with higher forms of black magic, and such things as drug addiction—yet we still consider it nothing more than a superstition or amusement. By the mid-1960s the Ouija board had surpassed Monopoly as America's favorite parlor game! It's like taking a bullhorn to a busy city street and shouting, "Anyone who wants to come home with me is free to do so." You may not like the person who responds to such an invitation.

The same is true of channeling and automatic writing, whereby spirits are allowed to use a human's voice or handwriting. This is dangerous in the extreme. Spirits are highly deceiving and can pretend to be "good" spirits, in the end causing tremendous bondage. Many are the "haunted houses" that are not haunted by ghosts as much as by the demonic imps that were channeled into a home through automatic writing or a Ouija board.

Is it really so dangerous? Saul (*1 Corinthians* 10:13) died, in part, because he consulted a medium for guidance. See also *Jeremiah* 27:9-10. In *Revelation* (21:8) we are warned that sorcery will lead to "the lake which burns with fire and brimstone." If that seems like folklore to you, let me assure you I have seen cases as bad as the townhouse in Chelsea that were caused by the same thing: necromancy, attempts to contact the dead. I saw a case in which a man felt smothered by a force that rolled on top of him and sent currents of "electricity" up and down his spine. Such close contact with spirits can take years to purge.

This is not to say that all such spirits are demons, for we are told, by mystics such as Padre Pio, that the deceased are occasionally allowed to appear to us, reminding us that they need our prayers to be freed from the agonies of Purgatory. But we should never seek to speak with the dead, and if a spirit plagues a home, we should pray for that soul and have a Mass said for its release heavenward. We should also pray that it isn't a demon in masquerade.

Demons try to lure us. They try to confuse us. They hunger for our attention, which feeds them power and places us within their orbit. They assume the voices of Jesus and Mary, especially to those whose pride immediately accepts them as a heavenly gift, without long and hard testing of the spirits.

Most insidious are the occult spirits that latch onto us without our ever knowing of their presence. Eventually we sense that something is wrong. Our relationships don't work. We are blocked in prayer. We are led to lust. We experience new negative emotions, like envy and superstitiousness. We see confusion, anxiety, and divisiveness.

When they are allowed to fester, these spirits can ruin us mentally and physically, and certainly spiritually.

They come through the occult. They come through games like "Dungeons and Dragons." They are swarming into our domain through the New Age. They dance to the tune of lesbian rock bands, or punkers who shout blasphemy. They come when they are called, when we rely on the occult instead of God; they come through the horoscopes now read by an estimated 70 million Americans. Even Nancy Reagan consulted an astrologer!

Such transgressions call out for God's chastisement and correction.

A nation which has turned to the occult is one which could expect the worst to come in economics and politics.

CHAPTER 24

Me and Hillary

Purge us all, oh Holy Spirit. Lead us to the proper way of deliverance, in obedience always to the Church. Guide us every inch of the way. Send us new battalions of angels. Send us the great Archangel Michael, and Saint Francis of Assisi, and the dragonslayer, Saint George. Deliver us from the energies that jump at us from social evils too numerous to name. Come, oh Lord Jesus, and break all bondage. Break the bondages of anger, sloth, addiction, pride, envy, promiscuity, gluttony, lust, resentment, unforgiveness, hatred, false prophecy, and the occult. Free us from unholiness of all kinds. Purge us of any demons we may have picked up. Let us not be deceived, oh Lord! Free us too, of any demonic forces that have come through the family tree. Free us of oppression, depression, discouragement, and every mental torment.

It's the second prayer of the warrior, the prayer of deliverance. For we must understand the effect of demons and that prayer is necessary to get rid of them. We must also understand how and why they come. One way was dramatically shown by an experience related by the great Francis of Assisi, who had a vision one day in which he saw his favorite place of prayer, the chapel of Portiuncula, besieged by devils—a great army. He watched them hover-

154

ing about the chapel but noticed that they were not able
to enter. They couldn't enter because the friars praying
inside were so holy.

However, soon one of the friars was stirred to anger with
a second friar and began thinking vengeful thoughts. As
Saint Francis watched, the protective grace around the
chapel was breached, the grace was lifted, the gate of virtue
abandoned, and the door of wickedness allowed the devils
in. They left only after the friar acknowledged his faults
and humbly asked for forgiveness, which once again points
up the importance of Confession and its power of
deliverance.

That is precisely how we are afflicted by demons:
through bad temper or unforgiveness or envy, which attract
evil spirits like dung attracts flies. Want a demon to latch
and sting? Try lying, cheating, stealing, or sexual
immorality.

They perch on us and sometimes are difficult to remove
without complete internal cleansing and prayers to the
Holy Spirit. So too can an entire nation, such as the United
States, find itself under a dark cloud because of its collective immorality. Besieged. Horribly besieged by high-level
demons. Besieged, but not defeated. No, America has
another chance. The world has another chance. Warnings
from God, such as those at LaSalette and Fatima, now also
Medjugorje, are usually conditional, meaning that a proper
response to such warnings will mitigate punishments. It
is an opportunity granted by Heaven and it reduces to three
words: *pray, pray, pray.* But the time has come to hurry.

"Without you I am not able to help the world," Mary
was saying urgently at Medjugorje. *"I want you to listen
to me and not permit Satan to seduce you. Dear children,
Satan is strong enough! Therefore, I ask you to dedicate
your prayers so that those who are under his influence may
be saved."*

While I was vaguely aware of Medjugorje when I lived
in Manhattan, I had no association with the Marian Movement. Most of my praying was done in private. Very private. Nearly in isolation. Once in a while I attended prayer
services with a Catholic or non-denominational charismatic

group. My mainstay was Mass as often as possible at Our Lady of Good Counsel, for it was there that I found the greatest consolation and protection, receiving the Eucharist.

I had moved to a walk-up building that was dark, like a hermitage, because they were turning the other place into co-ops, and I refused to pay the exorbitant price. Money, money, money. Manhattan now knew only MONEY. The dollar bill was idolized as never before; on it is even the symbol of a pyramid and all-seeing eye—reflecting back to ancient sorcery.

There had been similar periods like this, especially during the Roaring Twenties, but now the materialism and waywardness were reaching an unprecedented crescendo and young people, once idealistic, with goals beyond simple income, saw only the bottom line. Bankers gutted corporations to raid the cash boxes, and greed became synonymous with success on Wall Street.

As I recall they even filmed parts of the movie *Wall Street* in my neighborhood. Flash and cash. Money talked. Donald Trump. Young kids in Jaguars.

There is nothing wrong with making money. It is how the money is used and viewed. It isn't supposed to be our most important goal in life, but that's what it has become. I continued to speak on the college lecture circuit about toxic wastes and noticed how dramatically the students had changed, from societal idealists to nothing but investment banking. I was also disappointed at corporate values. At *Science Digest* we hired a Harvard heart specialist to test food samples from major hamburger chains for a story of mine on how beef tallow, which is terrifically high in fat, was being used by some of those fast-food chains to fry chicken, fish, and French fries. What we found caused a national stir. *The New York Times* ran an editorial urging changes in unhealthy frying practices and my article was reprinted as far away as Italy. I got letters from corporate executives who finally announced changes in those frying practices.

I also had begun working on the book I mentioned, *The Toxic Cloud.* I was concerned that chlorinated hydrocarbons were circulating at long distances, altering the biosphere.

Pollution is another manifestation of evil. A witch's brew! On the southeast side of Chicago, and down in Baton Rouge, and over in Texas and California, as well as north-central Michigan, I found disturbing indications that people—many people—were being harmed by airborne toxicants. I saw cases of babies born with anencephaly (unformed brains), and poor sharecroppers who lived near belching incinerators and suffered asthma, emphysema, and cancer. I remember one poor old guy whose wife had recently died after a release of noxious smoke from a stack at a particularly awful waste site in Baton Rouge. I recall approaching the place with a crew from *The Today Show* and noticing a small, dark, and very peculiar cloud hanging there low and alone, precisely above the area of contamination.

I also traveled around the world for a short picture-book on the history of the controversial environmental group, Greenpeace. It was done for a London publisher, and I conducted research in England, Paris, Madrid, Amsterdam, Goteborg, Copenhagen, Hamburg, Vancouver, Auckland, and Washington. Greenpeace was a fascinating group, but I became increasingly concerned with the New Age-like philosophies and radical politics creeping into the environmental movement.

While I was in England, working in the ancient town of Lewes, I had a memorable experience during Mass at an old church dedicated to the Archangel Michael. It's hard to express the power of the experience. During the peace exchange, an old woman in the pew in front of me—a woman who somehow reminded me of that inexplicable woman on Third Avenue, who had stopped me to make the sign of the Cross years before—turned around and gave me a beautiful smile. When she touched me I felt a wave of peace unlike anything I had ever felt at Mass—a feeling of peace that I would not experience again until I visited Medjugorje. So similar was she to the woman on Third Avenue that I yearned to find out who she was.

But I was in a hurry, on the move, working my way from country to country, and increasingly concerned about the environmental movement. It was becoming too secular:

everything was secularized. Or there were strong whiffs of paganism. I learned, to my discomfort, that one of Greenpeace's earliest members had been a long-haired hippie in Canada who used drugs, astrology, and the *I Ching*. Greenpeace drew its inspiration (not to mention much of its motif) from a book of Cree Indian prophecies called *Warriors of the Rainbow*. Back in the early days, Greenpeacers on an anti-nuclear protest voyage were anointed by Kwakiutl witch doctors.

The superstitions hardly qualified Greenpeace as an occult organization, and many of its members eschewed the earlier eccentricities, but there remained strong links to ancient mystery religions. Many of its members believed the 200-year-old Cree prophecies, which stated that "warriors of the rainbow" would rise to save earth once its land was fouled and water contaminated, were finally being fulfilled by Greenpeace. Among Greenpeace's "warriors" was Miriam Starhawk, the most prominent priestess on the earth-goddess circuit. Starhawk gave workshops on witchcraft and its relationship to ecology (teaching dozens of priests) participated in several of Greenpeace's protest actions, including demonstrations at the U.S. Defense Department's Nevada Test Site, Vandenberg Air Base, and Cape Canaveral and taught at an institute run by the renegade Dominican priest Matthew Fox.

Disturbing indeed. The New Age had many heads. It was a hydra. I found myself feeling increasingly isolated in the world of secular journalism. I was supposed to consider groups like Greenpeace heroic, but there was much about its spirit that I simply could not warm to. I discussed it with a few of them. I discussed God with David McTaggart, the international chairman, but he was an atheist and like my dwindling friends in the media, many environmentalists saw organized religion and particularly Christianity as the enemy. They felt it was best to have no beliefs at all, but if you were going to dabble in spirituality it should be paganism. The very symbol Greenpeace used was a rendition of a peace sign, the upside-down broken cross.

Alone. I was in isolation. I was in the most populated city in America, and now it seemed like I knew hardly anyone. As my Christianity developed I felt increasingly alienated from editors at the major magazines. I felt antsy visiting *The New York Times.* It seemed like a cave: dark and oppressive. And its editorial policies were highly anti-Catholic. *The Times* is a great source of news but also a great promoter of abortion and homosexuality (its foundation even funds the National Lesbian and Gay Journalists' Association), with no room on its opinion pages for contrary views. It seemed like the only time it reviewed religious books was when the book was New Age or had to do with problems in the priesthood. Born-again Christians were treated as eccentric and possibly dangerous, while homosexuals were handled with the highest respect, even those who belonged to the radical and blasphemous group called ACT-UP.

The Times is the definition of secular humanism.

And that left me cold. When I had lunch with an editor, things no longer gelled; it was like they could now detect something about my spirit they didn't like. There was a subconscious clash. Once highly complimentary about my work, they would soon rail against my next book.

It was a spiritual antagonism and I felt increasingly driven from the secular world. It was like a force was separating us. To me the existence of evil was starkly apparent, and yet none of the media so much as acknowledged its existence. Belief in evil spirits belonged to Pat Robertson or Jerry Falwell, who *The Times* and other newspapers barely tolerated as thinking humans.

The type of story the media most enjoyed was the scandal breaking across the Christian scene in the form of Jim Bakker and Jimmy Swaggart. This was around the time Bakker was found bilking television viewers while Swaggart, who despised the Virgin Mary, would soon be caught patronizing a street hooker in New Orleans.

It was a difficult time, and I didn't like the way America was changing. There was a coldness that was nearly reptilian. I couldn't believe how little people cared about toxic pollution; I couldn't believe how self-serving many politicians had become. I couldn't fathom their spiritual blindness. Where once my books were endorsed by people like Jane Fonda and Congressman Henry Waxman, I now

wanted little to do with them. While I was grateful to Waxman, chairman of the House subcommittee on health and
environment, for endorsing *The Toxic Cloud,* I soon
learned that he favored research into the use of fetal tissue
for medical procedures—something I found distasteful
beyond words, like Nazi genetic experiments.

What was the world coming to? What was *America* coming to?

Cold. It was a country that now looked upon everything
mechanically and with frigid selfishness. America had
become one big Manhattan. Pride was absolutely rampant.
I don't like to single out individuals, but during *The Toxic
Cloud* I had a memorable experience while researching two
toxic scandals in Arkansas. I learned that high levels of
dioxin-related compounds had been left exposed to the
environment of Jacksonville despite serious health com-
plaints from the citizens, including the death of a baby
whose liver and kidneys had accumulated chlorophenols
at up to 508,000 parts per trillion—in the same range as
dirt from Times Beach, Missouri, where hundreds had been
evacuated years before. Dioxin was even detected in the
air—something that had not happened at Love Canal! Vegetation was mutated, and birds would fly through and die
on the spot, littering backyards.

Yet the state was doing just about nothing.

In another town, El Dorado, residents feared that emis-
sions from a PCB incinerator might harm their children.
Once more, the state was doing nothing, which I found
very peculiar. In fact, so suspicious of state government
were the residents that they appeared willing to raise their
own money for a health study rather than trust the state
to conduct one.

There was something wrong in Arkansas. While the
citizens and county government were *fighting* the chemical
company, which had left Minnesota after a major environmental problem, the state itself was unusually supportive
of the company. I heard reports in 1986 that the outfit was
very friendly with the governor, and that his wife was a lawyer whose firm represented it. I also heard that the very
desk in Governor Bill Clinton's office was an antique on

loan from a company owned by the wife of the incinerator company's chief executive, Melvyn Bell.

I made a call looking for Governor Clinton, but he wasn't home, said a woman who answered the phone.

That was okay; I wanted to speak with her also. I wanted to know if it was true the governor was a friend of Melvyn Bell, and I also wanted to know if she represented the company as a lawyer.

Her attitude was incredible. Sure he was a friend, she said; he had just given $8 million to the local university's engineering school the previous Saturday. Sure he was a friend, and what are you going to do about it?

That was the essence of our conversation, which lasted only a few minutes. I was stunned by her audacity and arrogance. I was appalled by her lack of concern. There were those kids out there! I had never encountered such haughtiness.

I was totally taken aback not just by the words but by the *feeling* that came through my telephone.

I don't normally talk to myself but I remember hanging up and standing by my desk, telling myself aloud, "I have just spoken to the most arrogant person with whom I have ever spoken."

That person, of course, was Hillary Rodham.

CHAPTER 25

The Prayer for Spiritual Wisdom

Cold. Secular. America was no longer a Christian nation. At least it wasn't according to the media, which downplayed or ridiculed the Pat Robertsons and Pat Buchanans while twice putting Shirley MacLaine on the cover of *Time* magazine.

Something was very wrong and getting worse. I wanted less and less to do with the secular media. Even those who didn't *believe* in spirituality could sense something new about me. Our spirits clashed. I was tiring of hiding my Christianity. I was tired of the comments from atheists or New Agers with whom I so often dealt in the publishing field. And they were tiring of me. They weren't going to give me any more credit, and I wasn't going to cow-tow to them, either. I knew there was another reality—a *vast* and exciting reality—that the media didn't acknowledge even though this reality was more important than anything in the material realm.

I knew that it was the only reality, the spirit world, that really counted once all the cards were in.

The media thought it was nuts but there was no lingering doubt in my mind that life on earth is a constant struggle between actual metaphysical forces. Good and evil are not just societal issues; they are not just issues of who is polluting what lake or who is stealing on Wall Street. Good and evil are not solely played in the sociopolitical arena.

No, it is a very personal issue. Demons and angels fight over every *person* and family. That is essentially the condition on earth. At each turn in life, every hour, often every waking minute, we are given two different paths of thought and action, good or evil, and when we make the wrong choice—which is usually the easiest or most immediately pleasurable choice—we attract forces of darkness.

Let me state before we go on that it is a mistake to blame everything on evil spirits. It's a mistake to delve too deeply into their workings. It's a mistake to become overly curious. This is touchy business, and no one can really claim they truly understand the incorporeal netherworld. It is often just speculation based upon the experiences of deliverance ministers and mystics, as well as the Bible and scholars such as Saint Thomas Aquinas. Those who become obsessed with demonology—in it for the sake of curiosity, and curiosity only—quickly fall into its snares.

Too, we must realize that many happenings or problems in life may have little or nothing to do with demons. Things *happen*. We get sick through simple biology. We suffer stress because of fatigue. We have mishaps and accidents.

Life is like that. There are trials and sufferings. There are also mood changes and emotional disturbances that may be more attributable to behavioristic factors or even diet than to anything spiritual.

It is a mistake to attribute all that is unwelcome or unfortunate in our lives to demonic forces. There are evils that are constituents of our very existence. There is evil in our weaknesses. There are evils caused by our flesh and misuse of free will.

But it is equally dangerous to think of evil as something abstract, or to regard demons as a personalized fantasy. It is deleterious to ignore their often powerful and determining influence. When we have knowledge, we have an advantage over such influences; when we know where they are, we attain certain spiritual power and freedom. If we recall, Pope Paul VI said it is "very important to return to a study of Catholic teaching on the devil and the influence he is able to wield." The Pope said that the evil which exists in the world "is the result and effect of an attack upon us and our society by a dark and hostile agent."

To ignore the existence and workings of evil is to shirk our Christian duty. Joseph Cardinal Ratzinger, the renowned theologian and cardinal prefect of the Sacred Congregation for the Doctrine of the Faith, reminds us of our *obligation* to minister deliverance. "Anyone who has a clear picture of the dark sides of the age in which we live sees forces at work which aim to disintegrate the relationships among men," the cardinal told journalist Vittorio Messori. "In this situation the Christian can see that his task as exorcist must regain the importance it had when the faith was at its beginning. Of course the word 'exorcism' must not be understood here in its technical sense; it simply refers to the attitude of faith as a whole, which 'overcomes the world' and 'casts out' the prince of this world. Once the Christian has begun to be aware of this dark abyss, he knows that he owes the world this service."

Before anything, we should look for the good, for the Christ, in everyone. In the long-term we must focus on that which is positive in people. But we must also not be naive.

In a world dominated by evil, it is essential to know the enemy and to realize that the enemy is not an abstraction. When the evangelists spoke of evil, says Cardinal Ratzinger, they had "not the least intention of speaking symbolically. Like Jesus Himself they were convinced—and so they were determined to teach—that what was involved was a concrete power and certainly not an abstract concept. A power by which man is threatened and from which he is liberated by Christ, because He alone is the 'stronger man' who can bind the 'strong man,' to use the words of the Gospel" (*Luke* 11:22).

And so we pray for wisdom:

Lord Jesus, as the strongest Man, please bind all spirits that come against us. Please open our spiritual eyes. Please set us forth to understand what we should understand. Please grant us proper spiritual wisdom. Teach us to be wise. Teach us how sin attracts demons, or is inspired by evil to begin with. Grant that we carry forth our Christian duty without undue curiosity. Teach us that the more we sin, the harder and colder we get, the greater is our bondage.

Sin, demons, bondage. I saw this myself. I saw it during charismatic deliverances. I saw how when we sin, we open ourselves to demonic spirits. I saw how they attach themselves to us. I saw how their influence and number grow the longer we wallow in darkness. I saw how smaller evils beget larger evils. I saw how demons hook themselves onto damaged emotions or sinfulness.

Cling. All of us are in a constant battle with spirits trying to *cling* to us. If we have been in darkness long enough, or have inherited them from ancestors, they are sometimes even rooted within our personages. They watch us just as guardian angels watch us—but always looking for an opportunity to tempt us and find another pathway inside. They attach themselves or infest our very beings, like an insidious virus, until we are delivered from them.

More than anything they deceive us. Another name for a demon is "deceptive spirit."

After my experience with the charismatics in New York I became increasingly interested in the phenomenon of deliverance. I read books about demonology and studied what the Christian mystics had to say. I was most impressed with the works of Saint Teresa of Avila, who is a doctor of the Church. Like most great figures in Church history, Saint Teresa spoke often and openly about demons—unlike many modern priests and ministers who, bowing to the secular world, now shun any mention of personal evil.

At the charismatic churches I heard accounts of demon-infested people leaping like wild animals when charismatics started praying over them, or frothing at the mouth, or writhing like snakes. Some of these folks were homeless, some were addicts, some were wealthy yuppies whose lives had been ensnared by a force they didn't understand.

"Come out, in the name of Jesus!" the charismatics

would command. "We bind you, Satan. We bind you, strongman. We bind you in the name of Jesus!"

It seemed very weird, but funny thing was, it often worked. People were set free. Drug addicts kicked the habit. Homosexuals were freed of their sexual bondage. Rich kids started donating their time and seeing beyond materialism.

The deliverance folks talked about spirits of darkness that found entrances through drugs and alcoholism, through jealousy and anger. They claimed we especially open ourselves with acts of illicit sex, which generate enormous binding powers.

But they also talked about the little ways we summon trouble: through unhealthy literature, or bad habits, or the wrong movies.

The vast majority of people have no inkling of how many times their lives and moods are influenced from spiritual realms. There are spirits that cause fear, there are spirits of doubt, there are spirits of lust, addiction, and other compulsions.

More than anything these days, there is the spirit of pride.

Once inside, such spirits can be tough to remove. And while inside they cause tremendous mood swings, anxieties, paranoia, mental blockages, and sinful tendencies. Given time enough to root, they can cause increasing stress and tension, until we develop noticeable and sometimes clinical abnormalities. Christ Himself was certainly cognizant of diabolical infestations that caused sickness and mental derangement.

Deliverance ministers call demonic problems caused by sin "capital" infestations. There are also infestations caused by emotional wounds that have never healed, or hurts that have not been forgiven. Forgiveness is a most powerful tool of deliverance, and we must let go of past slights, rejections, or insults before we attain full spiritual freedom.

Almost everyone needs some form of deliverance, and deliverance does not have to be flamboyant and dangerous combat. It can be done softly and quickly, especially if it is done in conjunction with Confession and Eucharist.

Confession is a key to deliverance. When we confess our sins we are acknowledging the evil we have invited into our lives, and we are renouncing that evil. Renunciation of evil does a simple and yet extraordinarily powerful thing; it breaks our bondage to the evil. Confession and prayers of purification, in which we specifically pray to break each bondage brought into our lives through sin, open the clear path to full joy and deliverance.

While we are all called to involve ourselves with deliverance, strong cases should be handled only in groups under the direction of an experienced priest or minister, especially cases that involve criminality, suicidal tendencies, or the occult. Canon law 1172 specifies that no one may lawfully perform an exorcism without the express permission of the local bishop. We are allowed to pray as Jesus taught for freedom from all evil, but we must seek Church guidance if specific cases are approached, especially serious ones. Spirits of the occult and criminal behavior are the hardest to expel, according to deliverance experts. The occult infestations are tough to root out because demons have been summoned by what the Bible calls abominations. The same is true of homosexuality and blasphemy.

There are many levels of demons, just as there is a hierarchy of angels. I mentioned before that they graduate from fallen angels to fallen seraphim and cherubim, but actually we don't know the order of power. We can only speculate. All the Bible tells us (*Ephesians* 6:12) is that we are wrestling with ''principalities, against powers, against the rulers of the darkness of this age, against spiritual hosts of wickedness in heavenly places.''

Thus we can be certain only that there are principalities, powers, rulers, and spiritual hosts, all under the control of Lucifer. There seems to be a command structure. According to some deliverance ministers, at the lowest rung are what I have previously referred to as spiritual gnats, scorpions, or fleas. I could also have described them as immaterial jellyfish: simple animal-like devils whose sole ability and function may be to administer a constant temptation, or ''sting'' us with a specific niggling anxiety.

If you'll recall, at Fatima a demon appeared next to the young visionary Francisco Marto. Poor little Francisco had been given a glimpse of a reality that other visionaries have also experienced. At Medjugorje, the visionary Marija Pavlovic said during a vision of Hell she saw a beautiful girl enter the flames, and when she came out she was an ugly beast.

A third Medjugorje visionary described people in Hell as "like grotesque animals, but unlike anything on earth."

I have no idea what level of demon Francisco encountered, nor can anyone be sure whether condemned humans, like Marija Pavlovic observed, return to earth to do damage. The speculation is that they probably do.

Other demons, the fallen angels, are described as batlike or snakes or mere shadows. They can take any form, and cause just about any form of negativity. The more we give in to them the more powerful they get. Some are booted out only through fasting and frequent reading of the Bible. Especially important is renunciation of sin through Confession, as well as reception of the Eucharist. The Eucharist has tremendous deliverance power!

Demons that afflict us on an individual level are usually referred to as "ministering demons." There are also demons of greater power, intelligence, and communicative ability that are assigned to us, our leaders, and our Church. They can cause more effects and communicate with each other at great distances, although no one really understands the interplay and hierarchy. "There's so little known of the angelic world," says Sister Nadine Brown, a deliverance expert from Omaha who directs a whole community of prayer-warriors called "Intercessors of the Lamb." "As far as we know there are nine choirs of angels. When the fall came, Scripture tells us that Satan took one-third of them with him, so we're quite certain he took some from each choir. And so there's a hierarchy just as there is a hierarchy of good angels."

If so the demonic range goes from the scorpions all the way up to fallen seraphim.

According to Carlos Pantoja, a well-known deliverance minister in the San Francisco area, the lesser demons are activated by higher forces, such as principalities and powers.

Where the lower-aspect demons haunt people, the powers and principalities oversee entire spiritual domains such as lust, witchcraft, and false prophecy. Or, they afflict entire regions and seek to influence political leaders. We remember the Book of *Daniel* (10:13) where it took an angel 21 days to arrive because he was withstood by "the prince of the kingdom of Persia"—until this angel called upon Michael for help.

Like I stressed, Michael's rank is actually believed to be far above that of the typcial "archangel." It is Michael who often accompanies the Virgin to sites of apparitions.

Thus we see that there are probably controlling demons with fiefdoms or principalities that own actual territory. Many are those who relate stories of occultists "claiming" neighborhoods or cities for Satan during their rituals. It is basically the reverse of holy consecration, as Satan again tries to reverse that which comes from the Lord. Some people believe that the mere activity of witches or satanists, or past practices of ancient pagans, can cast a lasting pall over a territory.

I wonder if what witches and satanists do is similar to curses said to have been placed on the tombs of Egyptian mummies.

I also wonder if it relates to stories of especially voilent hauntings on or near Indian burial grounds, where there were pagan rituals.

Was that why some places seemed to be functioning with bad fortune: under a "dark cloud"?

We also hear charismatics speak of generic demons. There are, some claim, several basic territories or kinds of spirits involved with witchcraft, controlling demons of the elements: earth, wind, fire. In short, these are the nature "gods" that New Agers and other pagans revere. There are also spirits of rejection, confusion, gluttony and greed. If we can actually break it down as such, it is as if certain demonic entities control emotions just as they control physical territory.

Lust. Anger. Jealousy.

That's why they call them "forces of dark." They try to discourage us and cloud if not totally obscure our vision.

Or they hook us to obsession. We become obsessed with money, emotional hurts, relationships, sexual tendencies, work, superstitions, and people in general.

There are spirits that attach themselves to neighborhoods or homes, spirits that attach themselves to specific rooms, especially rooms where poignant sin has occurred, and even to objects, especially occult books or jewelry.

Summoned by a medium or Ouija board—or by a false visionary—they are able to impart superhuman knowledge of events happening far away, or events that may occur in the immediate future.

They dispense this knowledge through pendulums, through Tarot cards, through clairvoyance or channeling.

When a New Ager channels, or uses automatic writing, he is allowing a deceptive spirit to control his hand or voice box. These spirits can be further imparted through improper laying-on-of-the-hands.

Once attracted to us, they cause progressively severe symptoms: deception, oppression, depression, obsession, and finally possession.

Possession is simply when a demon of whatever level gains what they seek all along: full control.

CHAPTER 26

The Prayer of Fearlessness

The glory of it is that we have Christ, Who according to *Ephesians* (1:21) is *"far above all principality and power and might and dominion."*

Even better is what He has bequeathed to us. *"Behold, I give you the authority to trample on serpents and scorpions, and over all the power of the enemy,"* Jesus said in *Luke* 10:18-19, *"and nothing shall by any means hurt you."*

We are free in Christ. A light comes into our lives, and when the light comes, devils flee.

We are already victorious. We are victorious because Christ defeated Satan 2,000 years ago. What we must do now is claim and reclaim that victory. What we must do is go through Christ and break the pretenses of deceptive spirits.

What a joy that is! How bright and clean is the world when it isn't clouded by the oppression of evil!

Dear Jesus, please lead us, please lead everyone in our families, to the correct route of deliverance. Oh dear Christ, oh Holy Spirit: please send us the right prayer companions and ministers. Send us what we need to know. Send us the gift of powerful prayer that we may be freed and unhindered. Free us from any fears!

The warrior must move forward with no fear. If there is anxiety, that means the devil has a piece of us and is feeding off that nervous energy.

When we fear the devil we give him power because fear of him is faith in his nefarious power.

Fear *attracts* demons.

We should be extremely careful not to ascribe everything or see every negative as a work of the devil. It is important not to become obsessed with demons. Like fear, obsession with them can serve to enhance their power.

Oh Holy Mother of God, please pray specifically for us that we do not get carried away, that we never look upon demonic forces in an unhealthy way, that we learn what we need about evil and then move on, keeping our eyes on your Son, instead of Satan, on Heaven and not the netherworld. And Mother, let us see our own pride and be rid of it so we do not serve or fear the Prince of Pride.

Every day, from the heart, I say several times this simple prayer: *"Lord, in the name of Jesus, let me focus not on the devils but upon the glory of You and the angels. Upon Your truth and glory, Lord!"*

It's an important prayer, for to become obsessed with evil is to train our eyes on the darkness instead of the Light.

Before we advance forward we must first pray to the Holy Spirit for total freedom from any fears or obsessions.

There are two extremes, equally unhealthy: those who see no evil at all, and are totally ignorant about the working of demons, and those, fewer in number, who see demons everywhere.

There is no reason to fear a New Ager, or an occultist, nor even a practitioner of black magic. Only if we sin and continue on a path of darkness, only if we remain ensnared in obsessions or bad habits, only if we are prideful, can the fiery darts truly penetrate us.

That's not to say we'll never be harassed again. Life is a continual struggle. We all have crosses to bear.

But the darts will pinch and then fall away from us. They'll fall away because we're wearing the breastplate of righteousness, the shield of faith, and the helmet of salvation. They will flee from our sword, which is the Word of God. They will flee from our humility.

The enemy's darts? We encounter them every day. You know how it is: Everything will be going well, and your mind will be happy and at peace, when suddenly an anxious thought will come flying into your head from nowhere.

Or the actions and words of someone will sting you, burn you, create aggravation or apprehension.

That's what demons are constantly poised to do: disrupt you and especially take away your peace and equilibrium.

Or tempt you. They will lead you away from discipline. They will make you too antsy or too busy to pray or to read the Bible. They'll lead you back to bad habits, or to unclean thoughts, or to confusion and doubt. Confusion and lust especially. Lust and arrogance, which really opens us to snares.

If we are not armed against them, and if we don't recognize their wiles or deceptions, then demonic forces can often fester within us and cause us to sin or lead us into discouragement.

It's a tremendous daily challenge. And it can be dealt with only through faith, humility, self-discipline, reading of the Bible, and prayer. These dark angels, hovering constantly, have a field day when we don't realize they're affecting us and often step up their harassment when they see us breaking their grip and moving closer to God.

But we have Jesus. They should be made to fear *us*. We should act with the Lord's confidence. Saint Teresa of Avila once wrote that she feared people who were intimidated by demons more than she feared the demons themselves. "'Oh, the devil, the devil,' we say, when we might be saying 'God! God!' and making the devil tremble."

They should be made to fear and obey us. And indeed they must obey commands made in the name of Jesus. If the Lord is powerful, said Saint Teresa—as she knew He is—and if the devils are His slaves—which they are (an article of the Faith)—what harm can they do to a servant of the Lord and King?

How can a true believer fail to have the fortitude to fight, and if necessary, to fight all Hell?

That train of thought transformed Saint Teresa into a prayer-warrior. She fought the good fight, and she fought it with Crucifix in hand. She fought with true humility. "I found I was another person," Saint Teresa wrote, "and I should not have been afraid to wrestle with devils, for with the aid of that cross I believed I could easily vanquish them all. 'Come on, now, all of you,' I said: 'I am a servant of the Lord and I want to see what you can do to me.' It certainly seemed as if I had frightened all these devils, for I became quite calm and had no more fear of them—in fact, I lost all the fears which until then had been wont to trouble me. For, although I used sometimes to see the devils, as I shall say later, I have hardly ever been afraid of them again—indeed, they seem to be afraid of me. I have acquired an authority over them, bestowed upon me by the Lord of all, so that they are no more trouble to me now than flies. They seem to me such cowards—as soon as they see that anyone despises them they have no strength left. They are enemies who can make a direct attack only upon those whom they see as giving in to them, or on servants of God whom, for their greater good, God allows to be tried and tormented. May His Majesty be pleased to make us fear Him Whom we ought to fear and understand that one venial sin can do us greater harm than all the forces of Hell combined."

If we are to fear we should fear only God. There are at least 41 references to the word "fear" in the Bible—nearly as many references as there are to "faith." The Lord wants His people to "learn to fear Me all the days they live on earth," we are told in *Deuteronomy* 4:10.

"Fear of the Lord is clean," says *Psalms* (19:9). "Fear God," says *1 Peter* 2:17. "Honor the King."

"Fear of God is the beginning of wisdom" (*Psalms* 111:10).

For when we fear God we realize His power, and we realize the seriousness of our struggle in life. We realize it and set ourselves on a course toward Heaven.

We fear Him out of respect for His power.

Fearing the devil, on the other hand, is taking from God what should only be His. "These devils keep us in terror," added Saint Teresa, "because we make ourselves liable to be terrorized by contracting other attachments—to honors, for example, and to possessions and pleasures. When this happens they join forces with us—since, by loving and desiring what we ought to hate, we become our own enemies—and they will do us much harm. We make them fight against us with our own weapons, which we put into their hands when we ought to be using them in our own defense. That is the great pity of it. If only we will hate everything for God's sake and embrace the Cross and try to serve Him in truth, the devil will fly from these truths as from the plague.''

It is a short and simple remedy—as so many spiritual truths are simple and direct. The truth will set us free. Satan is a lover of lies, Saint Teresa reminds us, and will have no truck with anyone walking in truth. It's when he sees our eyes darkened—with confusion, with hatred, with anger, pride, or ego—that he gladly adds to our vanity and blindness.

The more we sin, the blinder we are to the spiritual dimensions.

The devil especially finds comfort in our pride and vanities.

Are we mired in pride? Do we think we are smarter or more spiritual than others? Do we judge? Are our egos easily riled? Are we concerned about status? Do we gauge a person's worth on a material or reputational basis? Are we jealous?

If so we must pray to free ourselves from any such pride, for a person free of pride, or at least free of most pride, is the toughest prayer-warrior.

The less pride we have, the less fear of evil.

A person rid of pride is a person of great discernment and strength.

A person of little pride is not easily deceived and is afforded special armor—special fearlessness—against the gathering enemy.

CHAPTER 27

The Second Prayer of Michael

That's the deeper, lasting spiritual advice. On a more immediate level, the mystics and saints tell how important the sacramentals are against evil assault. When Saint Teresa was attacked by the demon which was causing tremendous suffering she asked for holy water because she knew that would put the demon to flight.

"They also flee from the Cross, but return," she wrote. "So holy water must have great virtue. For my own part, whenever I take it, my soul feels a particular and most notable consolation. In fact, it is quite usual for me to be conscious of a refreshment which I cannot possibly describe, resembling an inward joy which comforts my whole soul."

The glory of breaking bonds and setting demons to flight: It gives us a clean, whole, and strong interior feeling. We should direct our prayers specifically at dispelling stress, depression, and anxieties.

I cannot overly stress the importance òf holy objects in the house, especially a crucifix in every room, and regular blessings by a priest. Spirits come and go and come again to disturb us. When we wear a Scapular or medal, we are afforded special protection. I recall how a demon once attacked Estelle Faguette, a mystic in Pellevoisin, France, but the Virgin immediately appeared to chase it away because Estelle was wearing the brown Scapular of Mount

Carmel. (*"Do you not see that she wears my livery, and that of my Son?"* Mary said to the demon.) I had my own experience when the dark entity appeared next to me and seemed to angrily reach to flick my Saint Michael's medal, so as to intimidate me not to wear it.

Holy pictures, blessed relics, and sacramental salt all carry a mysterious and nearly tangible power of protection. Neither can I overstress the importance of the Rosary, and *most* importantly, the Mass.

There is no prayer more powerful than the liturgy. It is a sacrifice. It's a deliverance. It's a healing. It's a worship service and supernatural rite all rolled into one. It is what Jesus asked us to do at the Last Supper. And I have no doubt, from a mystical perspective, that the Eucharist is imbued with the Real Presence, for receiving Communion in the midst of an attack causes the same flow of grace Saint Teresa mentioned.

Christ is inside us, and the more we allow Him in, the less any adverse spirit wants to enter. Daily Mass, or at least regular attendance, is vital in these times of great spiritual turbulence. Praying for deliverance in a small group before Mass, or even praying over someone, during special services, as he or she is standing before the Host, can be very powerful in deliverance. It would help if priests began specific healing and deliverance Masses. We should prepare for Mass by praying to the Holy Spirit, and have hearts full of thanksgiving afterward. Communion transforms us. It is truly manna from Heaven. It sustains us. It gives us life. It gives us courage.

Novenas and devotions such as that of First Saturdays are also key steps toward liberation. I remember a time when I was in between projects and didn't know what to do next. I was worried about income, as always writers fret about income. I decided to do the First Saturday devotion in order to continue my purification: Confession, a Rosary, and Mass on the first Saturday of the month for five straight months. At the end of the devotion I was offered an advance of $50,000 by Harper & Row for the book on toxic air pollution. That night, in joyful thanksgiving, I read the entire *Psalms*, expecting nothing else. However, the next day, to my surprise, the publisher increased the advance by $20,000.

I also found it advantageous to praise God in tongues when attacks were hot and heavy, or to say one hundred Our Fathers. Heavenly praise evokes the Holy Spirit, as does reading passages from the Bible and meditating on them. Over and again: *Praise God, praise God, praise to you, Lord Jesus Christ.*

Call upon the Virgin. Call upon Saint Joseph. Call upon Padre Pio and Saint Teresa and Saint Francis. Call upon Saint George. As it says in *Ephesians* (6:18), "praying always with all prayer and supplication in the Spirit, being watchful to this end with all perseverance and supplication for all the saints."

Call upon the angels: *Come, ye hosts of Heaven. Come and surround me and my family. Come, ye angels. Come, ye archangels. Come, ye dominations and powers and principalities and thrones and virtues and cherubim and seraphim of Heaven. Come and swarm around us, so that your counterparts from Hell may not approach.*

These prayers work. They invoke powerful forces. They protect and deliver. The angels!

One Saturday night at Elaine's, the famous restaurant on Second Avenue, I was feeling especially alone and isolated. My old friends had fallen away. And this restaurant which once seemed so exciting, the hub for the L.A.-New York jet set, now seemed dark, hostile, and repressive.

I was thinking about how dark it seemed when suddenly, at the ceiling near the pay phone, I had this incredible visual impression. I call it an "impression" because I am not a visionary. As with other experiences you will soon read, you should consider this a private observation and discern its authenticity. For several minutes I stared toward the spot near the ceiling because I could nearly see hundreds of tiny angels, as if pouring into that place from a hidden dimension. I didn't really see them, and yet I can still "see" the scene in my mind. It was clear and yet not clear, a cross between a mental vision and something that is physcially perceptible.

I have no idea what if anything it meant. But I can speculate that it was a little gift showing that where there is darkness, there is also the availability of angels—no matter how thick the darkness is.

Here I was in the buzz of Elaine's, the biggest celebrity place in New York, about a block down from where I lived, and I was "experiencing" angels. Call it an *impression.* I saw them—vague yet real—but I didn't really *see* them. Like outlines of tiny cherubim entering our world. While demons are rushing onto earth, so too are angels to defend us. We should especially remember that the chief prince, Michael the "archangel," must be more powerful than the devil, for it is he and his angels who cast Satan from Heaven (*Revelation* 12:7-9).

Most glorious prince of the Heavenly armies, Saint Michael the Archangel, defend us in our battle against principalities and powers, against the rulers of this world of darkness, against the spirits of wickedness in the high places. Come to the assistance of mankind whom God has created to His likeness and whom He has redeemed at a great price from the tyranny of the devil. Holy Church venerates thee as her guardian and protector; to thee, the Lord has entrusted the souls of the redeemed to be led into Heaven. Pray therefore the God of peace to crush Satan beneath our feet, that he may no longer retain us captive and do injury to the Church. Offer our prayers to the Most High, that without delay they may draw His Mercy down upon us; take hold of the dragon, the old serpent, which is the devil and Satan, bind him and cast him into the bottomless pit so that he may no longer seduce the nations.

CHAPTER 28

Ciao Manhattan

I left Manhattan in the spring of 1988. I couldn't bear the spirit there any longer. I started to feel evil not just when I passed the corner prostitute or wino, not just down in the Village or Times Square, not just when I passed a fortuneteller, but when I was around materialistic types, atheists, or those with any involvement whatsoever in astrology or the occult.

At parties I became terrifically uncomfortable when anyone used the name of Jesus in vain, or when anyone told the same kind of off-color jokes I used to find very funny.

I didn't like the loss of dignity. Evil attempts to rob us of our humanness and dignity. It strips the dignity from a woman who poses in a nudie magazine, and from a promiscuous woman who resorts to the bar scene. It strips the dignity of men who see nothing but flesh, and who see holiness as a weakness.

Nor was I happy with the way Manhattan was affecting the rest of the country. It was exporting ruthlessness and lust. It was institutionalizing the rebellion of the Sixties. Sometimes it seemed there were more people "living together" (practicing fornication) than there were married couples.

And many who did marry didn't want families. The "Me Generation" meant just that; children were not to get in the way of career advancement and the pleasures of a new and sensual era. They felt life on earth is not meant to be an arduous path, a struggle toward God, but rather one long pleasure trip. That was the new philosophy of America's popular culture. Although in quieter fashion, leftists continued to chip away at institutions that represented the stodgy old "establishment."

In addition, New York was at the epicenter of something that had all the earmarks of a biblical plague. It is called AIDS. And it seems like a ringing confirmation of the rising evil. Although the media immediately jumped on anyone who so much as hinted that AIDS was a warning from God, part of the beginning chastisements, that is precisely what it is. Like any chastisement, there are also innocent victims, but the fact remains that the vast majority of male cases, about 91 percent, involve sodomists or intravenous drug users.

If that isn't a site-specific chastisement, I don't know what is.

Shortly, when we analyze what else may be coming in the form of chastisements, the AIDS epidemic will appear in clearer context, as will the extraordinary prophecies of LaSalette. *"The earth will be struck by calamities of all kinds (in addition to plague and famine which will be widespread),"* Our Lady had said in 1846. *"There will be bloody wars and famines, plagues and infectious diseases."*

In *Exodus* God tells His people that He sends plagues so *"you may know that there is none like Me in all the earth."*

Those who feared God's word among the servants of Pharaoh regarding the warning, were spared a great storm of fire and hail. Those who didn't, suffered the same fate we now see suffered by the poor misdirected souls with AIDS.

No one can question the morality of homosexuality. It is wrong, period. The Bible leaves absolutely no doubt of that. "Neither fornicators, nor idolaters, no adulterers, nor homosexuals, nor sodomites, nor thieves, nor covetous, nor revilers, nor extortioners will inherit the kingdom of God" (*i Corinthians* 6:9-10).

What could be clearer? In *Romans* (1:26-27) Paul mentions "vile passions" such as the men who "burned in their lust for one another, men with men committing what is shameful, and receiving in themselves the penalty of their error which was due."

What a plague AIDS was becoming! Thousands of sensitive and intelligent young men were wasting away, their immune systems destroyed, their lungs full of pneumonia, their skin covered with horrible brown lesions and blisters known as Kaposi's sarcoma.

They were turned from handsome young men, many of transcending talent, to human wraiths.

The obituary page in *The New York Times* was filled with young designers, artists, singers, playwrights, novelists, photographers, decorators, dancers, and actors who were succumbing to the disease.

When I first heard of AIDS I figured it would transform the culture. I figured that homosexual men would change their sexual inclinations. After all, what rational human would risk a death sentence for a few minutes of unnatural sex?

This wasn't syphilis. This wasn't gonorrhea. This was fatal.

Yet instead of changing their lives these men continued on an extraordinarily promiscuous path, sometimes sleeping with four or five different men a week, and claiming 1,000 lifetime sex partners. They then blamed this disease on the Church, the government, and the rest of society.

They railed with special venom against Cardinal O'Connor, who opposed promotion of condoms and issued a simple truth: "good morality is good medicine." If the homosexuals followed Church teachings, there would have *been* no epidemic. It was as simple as that, but radical gay groups like ACT-UP couldn't stomach the truth. Before I left New York I watched with dismay as they stood with their backs to the altar during the entire Mass at Saint Patrick's, as a protest against the Church's teaching about morality. And that was nothing compared to what they did on December 10, 1989, when they stormed the cathedral during 10:15 a.m. Sunday Mass. Forty-three were arrested inside the church and 68 outside, among 4,500 protesters who were there (as *New York* magazine recounted) "to assail and mock the cardinal. Demonstrators outside dressed as clowns and bishops and wielded a condom the size of a giant torpedo labeled CARDINAL O'CONDOM. One man dropped by dressed as the Flying Nun." Some protesters chained themselves to the pews or blew whistles. They also shouted pro-abortion slogans. It was the beginning of a curious alliance: homosexuals and pro-choicers, with a common theme: down with traditional family values and sexual morality.

One man scrunched a consecrated Communion wafer in his hand and dropped it to the floor. Another man, John Wessel, a former Jesuit seminarian and regional director of the National Endowment for the Arts, broke the Host and flung it over the heads of the congregation.

It should have been no surprise that an official of the NEA would be involved. It was that government agency which presented a grant to Andres Serrano, the "artist" whose exhibits included a photo of Christ on the Cross submerged in Serrano's urine. (The title: "Piss Christ.") The NEA also directly and indirectly (through the New York State Council on the Arts) subsidized Chelsea's Kitchen Theatre, whose sensation was Annie Sprinkle, a porn actress (150 films to her credit) who conducted live sex shows for the theatre. ("Usually I get paid a lot of money for this, but tonight it's government funded," she commented.)

During the attack on Saint Patrick's, pro-choice and gay-rights activists wore gold colored robes similar to clerical vestments, and hoisted a large portrait of a pornographically altered frontal nude portrait of Jesus. "Eternal life to Cardinal O'Connor NOW!" screamed the placards. "Keep your rosaries off my ovaries."

No wonder that afterward Cardinal O'Connor felt the need to perform purification rites at the cathedral.

Up in Boston, meanwhile, a homosexual newspaper carried the ad of a black-clad man holding a condom above a Chalice.

Soon *The New York Times* carried a two-page ad for the play "Nuns on the Run," described as "The Funniest Anti-Clerical Transvestite Comedy of the Decade."

They called it the beginning of a cultural war, but really it is a spiritual war, and Manhattan is at ground zero. This great city, this city I had so loved, this city of so many wonders and good people, is in the throes of moral disintegration—a harbinger for the rest of the nation. Poor Cardinal O'Connor, attacked by AIDS activists despite the fact that he had worked long and hard as a humanitarian volunteer, visiting, washing the wounds, or emptying the bedpans of more than 1,000 people with AIDS.

The homosexuals didn't care about that. They knew only that the cardinal was opposed to their precious sodomy. The gays allied themselves with feminists who supported not just abortion but also lesbianism. It was an utter rebellion against traditional sexual mores. Both homosexuals and feminists shared a total and almost vindictive disdain for the traditional nuclear family. "Marriage has existed for the benefit of men; and has been a legally sanctioned method of control over women," said "The Declaration of Feminism" in 1971. "We must destroy it...We must go back to ancient female religions like witchcraft."

Okay, they were finally being honest. Like so many things, feminism and gay rights were rooted in debauchery and paganism. They weren't alone. It was open season on Christianity. In Wisconsin a group called the Freedom from Religion Foundation would soon try to remove Gideon Bibles from hotel rooms—declaring that the good Book made "gruesome, unsavory bedtime reading."

By the year 2000, said feminist Gloria Steinem, "I hope we raise our children to believe in human potential, not God."

It was time, said the radical feminists, to "forget about the mythical Jesus" (see *The Humanist*, July/August, 1988).

No wonder God was sending a plague. And a plague it was. By the end of the epidemic's first decade there were at least 110,000 Americans dead of the disease, far more than had died in Viet Nam. No one was quite sure all the ways this virus could spread, and there were signs that AIDS patients were carrying tuberculosis, which can be transmitted through the air. Yet there was no quarantine. AIDS became the first fatal infectious disease with special

civil rights. We didn't even have the right to know who
had it and who didn't. Not perverted sex but society was
to receive the blame.

In Africa, where the Virgin Mary had been appearing in
Kibeho, Rwanda, since 1982 (warning against promiscuous
sex), the plague was striking males and females in nearly
equal number. Entire villages would soon be decimated. By
some accounts 19 percent of the sexually active people in
Uganda alone were infected with HIV—up to 1.5 million out
of the nation's 18 million population!—and scientists were
baffled at why it was striking so hard at heterosexuals in
other parts of Central Africa as well, when usually AIDS
targets homosexuals. One reason for the epidemic in Africa,
perhaps, was the widespread practice of ingesting blood
during black magic or *juju*, which is also prevalent in
AIDS-ravaged Haiti. ''Recognizing ritual bloodletting as an
additional source of exposure to contaminated blood makes
the rapid and widespread distribution of HIV throughout
Central and West Africa not only understandable, but
inevitable,'' notes former juju high priest Isiah Oke.

So once again there were certain occultic roots, along
with the unnatural sex and selfishness. Most ominously, 34
of 132 sexually active respondents in one American survey
said they would not tell a casual sexual partner if they had
tested positive for the AIDS virus.
We were now in the age of viral manslaughter.
Selfishness had rarely reached such depths. It was
spiritual insanity. Yet gays found themselves backed
strongly by powerful newspapers such as *The New York
Times,* which relegated the Saint Patrick's debacle to a dis-
crete inside page.
The Times was hostile to Catholicism, and especially to
claims of the supernatural. It was okay for radical protesters
to blaspheme Mary and Jesus, but if any similar disruption
had occurred in a non-Catholic setting, especially if the
transgressors were Christians, it would have received large
and damning publicity.

Catholics were fair game. They were to be humiliated and
forced into accepting a new morality even though that

morality had been condemned by the Bible for thousands of years. There was no more need for the Bible. *The Times* was the Bible. This was the Age of Sexual Enlightenment. Everything in the past had been medieval gibberish.

It was irrational and demonic, a great victory for Satan, who manifested through gay and pro-choice activists when they held up placards mocking Jesus or His mother. ("The Madonna lusts Jesus!" shouted one lesbian "singer" at a later protest in the nation's capital.)

I'm sorry for being so graphic, but we must bring the evil into light. Ignoring it allows it to germinate in the dark like a fungus. Don't get me wrong. I don't dislike homosexuals as individuals, but it's impossible to approve of what they do. I've known homosexuals in publishing and they have been sincere, hard-working, caring people, quick to compliment your work and sensitive to the nuances of writing. But there is that side of them that is contrary to the Spirit, and I must write about it, however much I hate to. Besides, we are told by Paul in his letter to the *Ephesians* (5:11) to "have no fellowships with the unfruitful works of darkness, but rather expose them. For it is shameful even to speak of those things which are done by them in secret."

Publishers would soon be printing books (like Madonna's *Sex*) promoting sado-masochism, and the influence of S&M was now seen not just in the shops that sold whips and leather, but in movies, fashion, music, magazines, and day-time soap operas, which were filmed in Manhattan. For her book, Madonna posed at the Vault, Manhattan's premier sadomasochism club, one of many such nightspots that sprang up just before or soon after I left New York.

Even before I left there was a posh nightclub on the Upper East Side that featured transvestite performers.

Nearly two centuries after he died in a mental asylum, the ghost of Marquis de Sade was resurrecting.

Were he alive today, noted the Associated Press, "the marquis might be enjoying the spoils of multi-million book contracts and movie deals."

CHAPTER 29

Last Appearances

I returned to my hometown, Niagara Falls, an old tourist and factory town with trying winters but unbeatable summers and autumns. Having been away for many years, I decided to spend time with my large family, which was also undergoing a conversion.

It was the beginning of a period during which I would experience tremendous phenomena. I will not try to convince you of what I saw or heard through interviews and investigations at 33 reputed apparitional sites throughout the world. Believe what you will. I myself am often highly skeptical of supernatural occurrences, and would expect you to feel the same way.

It was also the period during which I became aware that the Blessed Virgin was issuing warnings in various parts of the world to mankind. Mary, it seemed, was appearing because of how dark the world had become. Aside from the brief magazine article I mentioned previously, the first thing I had seen about Medjugorje was a home video. The tape had been reproduced so often its quality was very poor. It was a VCR recording of various footage. There were several tapings on the video, including a couple of amateur documentaries about the supposed apparitions in the Bosnia-Hercegovina region of Yugoslavia and a snippet from the *Sally Jessy Raphael Show.*

187

The documentaries, one in particular by a priest named Edward Serena, were electrifying. I mean, as soon as I saw the faces of those Croatian teenagers, their eyes all trained on the same spot, their reactions simultaneous, a sort of glow imbuing their complexion—as soon as I saw that, I knew something extraordinary was at work. I knew this not just because of the way everything looked, but more because of how I *felt*. I felt as if a heavenly grace—an extraordinary peace, like what I'd felt after long sessions of prayer, praise, and tongues—was coming right out of the television and engulfing me.

Tranquility.

The Holy Spirit.

Mary.

The experience was all the more intense when I heard mention that these visionaries had been given "secrets" concerning the future—by implication the future of certain countries, perhaps the entire world.

Amid the overwhelming peace and grace that flowed from this place called Medjugorje was also an ominous undercurrent.

Those secrets supposedly contained information on events that would be sent by God as warnings and chastisements, along with a great sign or miracle.

The idea of these secrets, these mysterious secrets, was immediately galvanizing to thousands of Catholics, bringing to mind the famous Third Secret of Fatima which was never revealed. I wondered if Medjugorje meant that the Third Secret involved physical cataclysms. It was claimed (but never confirmed) that during a visit to Germany in November of 1980, at the square of a cathedral at Fulda, Pope John Paul II was asked about the Third Secret by a group of pilgrims and said it had not been released because it would "encourage Communists to take certain steps" and because the Vatican did not want prophecy mixed with sensationalism. Supposedly the Pope also commented that "if it is a question of a message where it is said that the oceans will entirely flood certain parts of the earth, that from moment to moment millions will die, hearing this, people should not long for the rest of the secret." The coming chastisements could be lessened, he said, if people responded to Mary's requests to return to God. Taking out a rosary, the Pope supposedly proclaimed, "Here is the remedy against evil. Pray, pray, and nothing more."

Whether or not there is the slightest truth to the claim that came out of Fulda, it was highly interesting in that years before *another* group of Europeans, this time from a weekly called *Neues Europa,* claimed to have intercepted a diplomatic cable that carried excerpts of the Third Secret, including the message that "the time of times" would soon come if mankind did not convert, "nay, if all becomes even worse." There was going to be a "big, big war" someday, claimed this 1963 article, and "fire and smoke will fall from the sky and the waters of the oceans will be turned to steam—hurling their foam skyward." It too said millions will lose their lives.

Roundly dismissed as phony, few accept the excerpt as the real Third Secret, and I have no idea what to think of something so very gloomy and sensational. I maintain skepticism. It was reported that Lucia dos Santos herself, who had personally received the Third Secret from the Virgin so many years before, indicated there was no truth to rumors such as the above.

In 1977, however, Radio Vatican had this to say: "Neither Pope John XXIII, nor Paul VI, considered it advisable to reveal to the world the third part of the mystery of Fatima. What has been published in the newspaper...*Neues Europa,* on October 15, 1963, has never been confirmed nor directly denied. However, there is a certainty that the Third Secret contains a particular gravity, confirmed by the tragic reality that the entire world is living today." The broadcast, as quoted by Ambassador Howard Q. Dee of the Philippines, also said it "is now necessary to act immediately if we wish that humanity, that each of us, may be able to see...besides the fire...the light."

There were glaring similarities between the *Neues Europa* text and the message from the Church-sanctioned site of Akita, including that "cardinals will oppose cardinals and bishops will oppose bishops." Cardinal Ratzinger, who, I repeat, had both read the Third Secret and approved dissemination of the Akita warning, hardly dismissed the magnitude of the secret. When pressed by the journalist Messori as to whether the Fatima secret also contained something "terrible," Ratzinger cleverly replied: "If that were so, that after all would only confirm the part of the message of Fatima already known. A stern warning has been launched from that place that is directed against the prevailing frivolity, a summons to the seriousness of life, of history, to the perils that threaten humanity. It is that which Jesus Himself recalls very frequently: 'Unless you repent you will all perish. . .' (*Luke* 13:3). Conversion—and Fatima fully recalls it to mind—is a constant demand of Christian life. We should already know that from the whole of Sacred Scriptures."

At LaSalette, where there had been equal controversy over Melanie's message, the bottom line was: *"Woe to the inhabitants of the earth! God will strike in an unprecedented way."*

While the LaSalette apparition itself had met with official Church sanction, the specific prophecies were not necessarily accorded similar approval. That was a separate issue, and anyway, it was difficult coming to grips—indeed, impossible to come to grips—with an actual time frame. LaSalette had occurred in 1846 and some of its prophecies were still slowly unfolding 140 years later. Would Medjugorje shed light on LaSalette and Fatima?

Perhaps, but the main message from Medjugorje was peace, faith, and hope. Mary was coming to tell us *how* to lessen punishments, and it meant conversion, fasting, penance, and prayer—urgently. The other key message is that God and the supernatural exist; and, yes, Satan does too. There's a war. And it's heating up.

Perhaps the most activating aspect of this place in the hinterlands of Western Yugoslavia was the incredible idea that the six visionaries—honest, simple, humble peasant kids—were seeing a three-dimensional, corporeal apparition, a virtually *tangible* apparition, of the Virgin Mary, mother of Our Lord, each and every day.

They were encountering a spirit from another reality called Heaven.

It was awe-inspiring, and nothing seemed staged. I played and replayed the tapes, especially struck by the visionary

Ivanka Ivankovic, whose face reflected a simple loveliness and an angelic luminosity. She looked like a no-nonsense type. She didn't look like any kind of fanatic. An everyday teenage Croatian peasant girl. Later, when I stayed at her pilgrim house, she spent long hours in her front yard shoveling fill; there was simplicity and humility, like Lucia, despite her world fame.

Then there was the youngest visionary, little Jakov Colo, not even a teenager yet, his head barely visible, craning his neck to look up at something invisible to the rest of the world.

In my heart, if not yet my intellect, I knew it was real. I was still living in New York City when I saw the video. I had been home on vacation. It was the summer of 1987, and my parents had received the video from a local priest, Father Alfred R. Pehrsson.

Immediately I had gone to see Father Pehrsson, a humble, level-headed man who already had been to Medjugorje. Father Pehrsson regaled me with his account of the "sun miracle," explaining that he had been able to stare at the solar orb for ten minutes without hurting his eyes or seeing sunspots afterwards. He said a sort of a disc that resembled the Communion Host moved in front of the sun's hot center (to blot out the most dangerous rays) while the rest of it spun and pulsed as at Fatima.

Father Pehrsson gave me some literature about the place, including a book by French Mariologist René Laurentin called *Is the Virgin Mary Appearing at Medjugorje?* I took it to my parents' house, and as I was walking in their backyard I decided to stare at the sun to see if it did anything.

It did not. It was the same old afternoon sun. But when I looked away, something extraordinary occurred. Instead of the normal sunspots—the black or gray dots you see after looking at the sun—I saw three or four rose-colored hearts floating across my field of vision. I watched them for several minutes. I was really seeing this. Several hearts moving across my train of sight. I knew then that I would soon travel to this place I could hardly pronounce, *Med-u-goree-a.*

Father Laurentin's book was fascinating. It contained interviews with the youngsters and in those interviews the visionaries exhibited a consistency and simplicity that argued compellingly for authenticity. The six kids were seeing or had seen (two by now no longer received daily visitations) something very out of the ordinary. What descriptions! Mary wore a gray robe, a white veil, and a crown of 12 stars—as in *Revelation.* She had blue eyes and black hair. Her cheeks were rosy and her feet hovered above the ground. She was 19 or 20. Her feet were in a cloud. She would arrive after three flashes of light and manifest as a real, living person. They could touch her! Speaking Croatian, she introduced herself as "the Blessed Virgin Mary." At the beginning of each apparition she said, *"Praised be Jesus."*

It was obvious that these experiences were taken with extreme seriousness by the youngsters, who had risked the wrath of local Communist officials to see her on the nearby hill. When they were in ecstasy the youngsters seemed like they were transported to another dimension. Another space and time. They were unaware of anything but the Virgin. Flashing cameras or pokes by examining priests did nothing to divert their mesmerized stare. At the end of the apparitions they said *"Ode"* ("She's gone") in perfect unity and rose to their feet from the altered state of consciousness.

They said the Virgin emphasized prayer, conversion, fasting, penance, and faith. As for the secrets, they had to do with the Church, with their own personal lives, and with humanity in general. There was also a message to the Pope, given to Vicka (pronounced *Vish-Ka*) Ivankovic. It was that he should consider himself the father of all people, not only Christians, and should tirelessly promote peace and love.

Mary identified herself as the "Queen of Peace" and on one occasion, August 6, 1981, the word *"MIR"* (Croation for "peace") had been seen by the villagers miraculously scrawled across the sky.

Everyone in the village seemed to be witnessing peripheral phenomena! So were the inflowing pilgrims. *"Peace, peace. . . nothing but peace,"* intoned the Virgin. *"Men must be reconciled with God and with one another. For this to happen it is necessary to believe, to pray, to fast, to go to Confession."* The seers were said to have been astonished when the Virgin told them there was a saint in the village. They were astonished because this person wasn't Catholic—was indeed Muslim.

"Members of all faiths are equal before God," Mary explained. *"God rules over each faith just like a sovereign over his kingdom. In the world, all religions are not the same because all people have not complied with the commandments of God. They reject and disparage them."*

According to Laurentin's book (written with Father Ljudevit Rupcic), the great Pentecostal leader David DuPlessis had visited Medjugorje and was deeply impressed, even though many Pentecostalists believe such apparitions are always a deception by the devil (which, for sure, they too often are). "For a long time I have been afraid of your Catholic tradition concerning Mary, because she does not occupy such a place among us," said DuPlessis. "Among you I have come to understand that Mary leads to Christ." He felt "the whole place is charged with the love of God. You can feel it, and you can see it. I told myself that if there had been anything wrong with what was happening here, there would not be the manifestations of the Holy Spirit that I could observe." His conclusion, thus, was that Medjugorje is "of God."

I found that exceedingly important. For years I myself had grappled with the issue of Mary—not due to any personal doubts, but because of the poison of criticism, true venom, leveled by certain non-Catholic charismatics and unaffiliated pentecostalists. I had loved those people and learned much from them, especially about deliverance, but like everyone else, like me, they were at times deceived, and I believe it was the devil who planted negativity in them about his great nemesis, Mary.

Now one of their greatest leaders, a man who, like so many pentecostalists, had a gift for judging spirits (known as "discernment"), was endorsing Medjugorje!

Why was there so little about Mary in the Bible?

That there is nothing specifically about her heavenly role in the New Testament is because that heavenly role came to be after she was assumed into Heaven!

While she was on earth Mary was the model of humility, and doing God's Will in all things.

She downplayed herself and always pointed to her son,

just as she now points to Him during her apparitions. *"Whatever He says to you, do it,"* Mary said at the wedding in Cana (*John* 2:5).

And right from the start at Medjugorje she made it clear that *"there is only one mediator between God and man, and it is Jesus Christ."*

Mary was a messenger, a harbinger, re-introducing Him as she had also been the first with knowledge of Him twenty centuries before. She was the woman mentioned in *Genesis* (3:15) and now, with the spinning sun and other solar miracles, she was coming as the *"woman clothed with the sun"* (*Revelation* 12). That was clear by the 12 stars she wore as sort of a hovering crown.

Mary pointed to the Gospels and said all the answers were in them. But she also had additional words of advice, and I was totally taken by her messages, which possessed a power of allocution—an economy of language functioning on several levels—which *in* that power were second only to biblical communication.

This was the real stuff. This was the height of Christianity. The main message was prayer and faith. Repentance. It reminded me of John the Baptist—'Repent, for the Kingdom of Heaven is at hand!" (*Matthew* 3:2)—and indeed the first apparition had been on June 24, 1981, feast day of John the Baptist.

"I have come to tell the world: God is truth," she said to a seventh young villager, Jelena Vasilj, who received not apparitions but messages or "locutions" in prayer. *"He exists. In Him is true happiness and abundance of life. I present myself here as the Queen of Peace to tell the world that peace is necessary for the salvation of the world. In God is found true joy from which true peace flows."*

What she told the visionaries about the world was especially intriguing. She predicted to Marija Pavolovic in October of 1981 that while Communism held Poland captive, eventually *"the just will prevail."* It was an unlikely prophecy that came true seven years later. Remarkably enough, she also said that *"Russia is where God will be most glorified. The West has advanced civilization, but without God, as though it were its own creator."* She

added on July 21, 1982, that *"prayer and fasting can pre-vent even war."*
"Prayer and fasting can suspend laws of nature!"

These were strong, strong words, and they went right to my heart. They went right to my solar plexus. I was taken by how frequently the Virgin mentioned Satan, just as the charismatics did. She even prayed like charismatics, with palms upward, and there were charismatics involved in the early days of apparition, including the local pastor, Father Jozo Zovko, who also preached about the devil.

I had never heard much mention of Satan in a Catholic context until reading about Medjugorje. The modernist priests stayed away from the unpleasant concept. This wasn't feelgood stuff! But Satan wasn't an artifact of the medieval imagination. He was real. He was very, very active. Recall, if you will, how the visionary Mirjana *saw* him manifest.

"According to certain Catholic experts who have studied these apparitions, this message of Mirjana may shed light on the vision Pope Leo XIII had," wrote another of the local priests, Father Tomislav Vlasic. "According to them, it was after having had an apocalyptical vision of the future of the Church that Leo XIII introduced the prayer to Saint Michael which priests used to recite after Mass up to the time of the Second Vatican Council. These experts say that the century of trials foreseen by Leo XIII is about to end."

The Church had indeed seen a century of tremendous persecution, first and foremost the onslaught of secularism, which in places such as America had taken anything to do with Christ out of public life, especially the schools. I think of my own alma mater, in theory a Catholic school but one that had become nearly totally secularized. I think of the Darwinism that replaced God as Creator, I think of the inventions that puffed man up with incredible pride. I think of our landing on the moon and telecommunications and lasers: Man was now himself reaching the point of "super-natural" miracles.

Turn on a switch and there on TV, a living picture!

And that was only the indirect persecution. There had also been massive holocausts under Lenin, Stalin, Khrushchev, and to a lesser but still significant extent Brezhnev and Andropov: Christians had been apprehended, beaten, and killed or incarcerated. Millions upon millions. As many as ten million Ukrainians may have been starved to death in the 1930s alone. Priests killed by firing squads or sent into the gulag for ten years just for hearing Confession or teaching the catechism. Baptists sent to Siberia. Evangelicals executed. By 1950 more than 4,000 Catholic churches in the Soviet Union had been destroyed or given to the state-run Orthodox, and the same thing happened in China and other Communist nations. Catholics, Baptists, and Pentecostalists alike were ruthlessly hunted down. So were many Orthodox. It was the greatest religious persecution in history—more martyrs this century than in all previous centuries combined. And it had all been predicted by the Virgin at Fatima, in 1917.

In other countries the faith was dwindling in less obvious but equally damaging fashions.

It was the hour of the red dragon, his final hour.

And now it was also the hour of the woman clothed with the sun.

She was in Medjugorje issuing very stern warnings. That was one of the most magnetic qualities of Medjugorje, part of its very essence. Mankind was in trouble, and needed to repent in a hurry.

Within the lifetimes of those visionaries, born in the mid-1960s, the events in the secrets would unfold.

There was talk of impending calamities.

The Virgin was saying that the world was heading toward perdition.

Humanism, occultism, scientism.

Man as creator.

It had all piled up to the point where heavenly intervention was necessary.

The music, the sex, the addiction, the immorality, the materialism, the break-up of families, the New Age. Did the sin of the world warrant punishment as in biblical times?

According to Mirjana, these would be the Virgin's last appearances of our era.

CHAPTER 30

The Sign of Jonah

I went to Medjugorje strictly as a pilgrim on May 16, 1989. It was night, the sky very unusual, like the clouds were shifting uneasily, a very strange and nearly eerie sky. The backlighting of the cumulus, from an almost full moon, was dynamic and spectacular, the light falling softly across an otherwise black horizon, full of quiet power, the dark night sky.

According to Mirjana, "these times would mark the Virgin's last appearances of our era. The sin of the world warranted punishment as in biblical times."

I had no idea what to think about that. When they spoke of our times as the "hour" of Satan, his final hour, I knew that "with the Lord one day is as a thousand years, and a thousand years as one day (*2 Peter* 3:8)." No one could say when the events granted in secret to the visionaries would commence, except that they would happen within the lifetimes of the Medjugorje visionaries, who, if they enjoyed an average longevity, would live until the year 2040 or so.

It didn't mean things were going to happen tomorrow or even this decade.

But there were already certain trends and events that I wondered about. The previous summer, America had encountered a highly unusual pattern of weather, with little rain and scorching temperatures, such that scientists claimed it was an indication of global warming, the result of gases we have injected into the atmosphere. The earth was getting hot, smoldering in its own fumes. It also seemed like the ocean was coughing back man's filth, for during that same summer beaches were closing along the East Coast due to garbage and bacteria.

Medical refuge washed onto shores, turning them into a health hazard.

While there remained little actual proof that the earth is in a trend of long-term warming, something did seem to be causing certain meteorological deviations, for soon after the declarations of global warming, other parts of the world reported *subnormal* temperatures, and it poured rain— belched rain—in areas that seldom see precipitation.

If it isn't just an era of momentary fluctuation, with effects caused by purely temporary factors like volcanic ash, it is a sign, perhaps, that greater fluctuations and then transformations will be seen in the near future. *"The seasons will be altered, the earth will produce nothing but bad fruit, the stars will lose their regular motion, the moon will only reflect a faint reddish glow,"* said the reputed message at LaSalette.

The Virgin added that the earth was *"asking for vengeance because of man."*

Before or soon after I traveled to Medjugorje there were a couple of other notable events. A major earthquake struck Mexico City, killing many thousands, and a Richter 7.1 quake rattled nothern California, including San Francisco, the hotbed of American New Age and debauchery. Who could really say, but they seemed like little pre-signs or pre-warnings. Little nudges. Little wake-up calls. On December 7, 1988, a Richter 7 on the troubled border of Turkey and the U.S.S.R. took 25,000 lives, while 50,000 succumbed two years later to an earthquake in the western region of Iran.

I wondered if slowly but surely, in graduated steps, hardly noticeable, a spiritual chastisement, already at great force in the invisible world, was manifesting through geophysical perturbations—if it was the onset of the wars, rumors of war, famine, and earthquakes that Christ (*Matthew* 24:4-12) called the beginning of sorrows. I saw a study conducted by Dr. Nelson Pacheco, a Catholic mathematician and computer scientist who had worked for the Air Force in satellite tracking and missile targeting, which maintained that indeed the *"birth pangs"* mentioned by Christ are upon us, in the form of all three factors: famine, war, and earthquakes, especially smaller tremors that according to this scientist have significantly increased in frequency. "This increase may be in part attributable to an increase in the number and sensitivity of seismographs located around the world," observed Dr. Pacheco. "However, that the number of recorded lower-magnitude earthquakes shows a local peak in 1986 argues that the cause for the rise is more than simply a larger number of seismographs."

Pacheco argued that, like tremblers, famines are also on a steady upward trend. He asserted that even the beleaguered 14th century, when Europe took the double whammy of famine and the Black Death, paled in comparison with both the 19th and twentieth centuries, which thus far have given us Somalia, Kampuchea, and Bangladesh, among other agonies associated with hunger. While Westerners fight to lose weight, plagued by too much fat, and squandering volumes of energy and food, much of the world experiences severe resource shortages.

Such imbalances, along with evils nurtured in the way of fanatical nationalism, would set the spiritual and psychological stage, I gathered, for hostilities and other forms of unrest in such places as the former Soviet Union. Already, according to Pacheco, who was employed by defense think tanks such as the Institute for Defense Analysis and the MITRE Corporation, there had been a "dramatic increase in major battles within the last two centuries." He displayed this in the form of a graph illustrating conflicts from the Peloponnesian Wars of 500 B.C. to the present, and that graph, based on information from "Brassley's Battles," the most comprehensive and authoritative list of hostilities ever compiled, showed a tremendous leap since the 18th century, such that the graph line is nearly in vertical trajectory. "Since World War II we have not had a period of sustained peace, but instead have been visited by nearly continuous battle," noted Dr. Pacheco, who believed mankind was entering highly unusual times, times of purification.

I knew such figures could be rebutted by those who saw a different point of view (and who therefore marshaled contradictory statistics), and I was aware that there had been massive battles in the long-ago past, making our era anything but unique in its warfare. Many millions were killed in 1644, for example, during the Manchu-Chinese War. Likewise, I knew that, proportionately, the Black Death, consuming a *third* of the European population, was greater than any similar recent tragedy.

I was aware in sorting through apocalyptical literature—"end-times" literature—that we must be careful not to prematurely anticipate biblical denouements, as so many have done throughout the past. For rare is the generation which has *not* expected final fulfillment of age-old prophecy. During the sixth century Pope Gregory wondered aloud if some of the signs forecast by Christ as signaling The End had not already materialized. There were nations rising against nations, and earthquakes overwhelming "countless cities." In the 13th century there were so many predictions of the world's demise that Saint Bonaventure openly complained about it, and toward the conclusion of the 14th century, during the great Western Schism, false seers rose everywhere, leading priests to sermonize upon baseless prognostications. Peasants and young girls, along with hermits, fell to political or religious prophesying at the beginning of the 16th century also, until Leo X published a bull prohibiting preachers from speaking of private revelations.

What they had failed to understand, those who jumped on prophecy and saw their era as the finale, is that "signs of the time" are given to every era and are pertinent to events designed to correct those *specific* eras, not necessarily—although this is always a possibility—to announce the End Times and the Coming of Christ. We can see the use of phenomena to warn mankind of impending judgments (not the Last Judgment, but contemporary judgments) in *Numbers* 16:30-37 and *Deuteronomy* 11:6.

Throughout the Bible, from *Daniel* to *Mark*, we are told that God sends us signs, that as *Hebrews* 2:4 puts it, God bears witness "both with signs and wonders," and by implication, every era receives its Heaven-sent omens because of the Hell-sent agonies. When Jonah failed to warn Nineveh of its evil ways, God made the seas tempestuous as a sign of His displeasure—and to nudge Jonah into warning Nineveh of looming chastisements if it did not repent. Throughout the ages natural phenomena have been associated with major coming events, events important to that specific era but *not* apocalyptical. I mentioned in the first chapter that a comet appeared in the sky in 44 B.C., the year that Julius Caesar was assassinated.

But our era is unique in several regards, first, in that it is experiencing a supernatural episode, focused on Medjugorje, that rivals anything since the Pentecost. This episode is full of ominous undercurrents and special warnings. Second, the level of defiance and immorality, which is the greatest sign of the time, has reached daunting heights. This tidal wave of unchastity has stripped even our children of their spiritual dignity and has subjected us to abortion and a new scourge, AIDS, that in sheer numbers—up to 40 million expected to be infected worldwide by the year 2000—may well one day surpass the bubonic plague.

We do not want to become a doomsday Church. No, that would be what Satan wants: to send us running for the hills, forming cults or sects of survivalism, instead of standing firm and fighting. But something is going to happen when even the youth are losing all semblance of innocence (see *Jeremiah* 32:32), and as God abandons us to ourselves, we can expect, as the likeliest prospect, a future just full of war and societal unrest. There is probably no better evaluation of our current times and the chastisements we face, no better prophecy, nothing more urgent for you to read in its entirety, which is a bit too lengthy to quote here, than the very first chapter, verses 1-31, of *Isaiah*.

"*Hear, O heavens, and give ear, O earth!*"

The childhood loss of innocence, that sure indicator of special times, is the result of an entertainment industry that has turned critically nefarious, pervading every American home and exposing the average youngster to 15,000 murders on television or at the movies before the age of 18. How right was Our Lady of Quito when in 1634 she told Mother Anne of Jesus Torres, in an apparition approved by the Church, that *"moral calamities"* would come during the twentieth century and *"the licentiousness will be such that there will be no more virgin souls."* In America about 200,000 children are now molested by other children each year, and nearly 4,800 kids under the age of 18 are arrested for rape. There are girls attacked in the school restroom while a teacher across the hall is lecturing on algebra. In England two teenage girls who the judge called "evil products of the modern age" stabbed a 70-year-old woman in the chest and face for the fun of it, while elsewhere in that same nation ten-year-olds were being arrested for homicide. There was a case cited by William J. Bennett, former secretary of education, of a mother forcing her daughter into prostitution to support a cocaine habit, and yet another involving parents who killed a baby by blowing cocaine smoke into the infant's lungs. "If that isn't the face of evil in our time," commented Bennett, "I don't know what is."

By the time they are 20, three-quarters of young Americans have had sex, and each year a quarter of all teens contract some form of venereal disease, according to *Time* Magazine. Among sexually active teenage girls, 61 percent have had multiple partners, up from 38 percent in 1971.

From whence comes their guidance?

Our culture is held hostage by "stars" like Sharon Stone, who became the first major actress I know to expose her most private parts (in *Basic Instinct*) on the silver screen, and who, according to a magazine called *Vanity Fair*, uses an occult mantra ("May the goddess enlighten me") during her seductive and lurid performances.

CHAPTER 31

The Dark Night Sky

It is a more important indicator than any war or famine, the rising, surging evil, and it has even infiltrated segments of the White House in the form of gay activism and lesbian appointments. Many are the lesbians who practice goddess worship and other forms of witchcraft.

"America gets a New Age president this week," said the inaugural coverage of Bill Clinton in *Newsweek* during 1993. "He can speak in the rhythms and rhetoric of pop psychology and self-actualization. He can search for the inner self while seeking connectedness with the greater whole." He also "talks from time to time in the lingo of 'centering' the personality and 'channeling' creative personal energy."

It is a true indicator of perilous times when proponents of abortion—active proponents—have assumed the national throne, or when a society, tinkering with life itself, moves toward genetic experiments and euthanasia.

So too, is it a sign of immense spiritual struggle when the enemy appears behind our lines of defense. It has become commonplace to read of Church scandal. The priest heading a home for wayward youth in New York was accused of seducing male youths seeking his refuge, and there was shame after shame involving altar boys. In Santa Fe and Atlanta, archbishops soon would be publicly disgraced for heterosexual scandals.

In America alone there were 51,000 priests, and if a few hundred had gone bad, in some cases very bad, or even a thousand, what was that, one or two percent of the priesthood?

A great world it would be if only one percent of the population had gone bad.

But no doubting the problems. The Church was in crisis. There was even a paternity dispute involving a bishop in Ireland. In a mere seven years fifty Canadian priests would face sex charges, while in my own parish a priest had left his vocation to become executive director of the local Planned Parenthood. Another priest would be investigated for a missing $500,000 in the next town over. Meanwhile the diocesan controller, a lay CPA who liked yachts, ended up in the penitentiary.

Satan is also behind our lines when he attempts to discredit the charismatic gifts by raising unnecessary doubts—turning priests and ministers into scoffers—or, failing that, by contaminating the true mysticism with erroneous tongues, false visions, bogus signs, or errant "words of knowledge," which do warrant skepticism. Rare is the ministry or diocese without a locutionist (some areas boast more than a dozen), while full-scale, corporeal apparitions—a far higher manifestation than mere locution—are being claimed in at least twenty American states, not to mention more than thirty foreign countries.

I don't doubt that a number of such revelations are worthy of some merit, and after dozens of interviews I concluded that at least three or four cases of alleged apparition in Canada and the United States warrant serious study by bishops' commissions.

But there are *hundreds* of others, similar to what happened at Lourdes where the bishop condemned a flurry of "false visionaries" who came onto the scene toward the end of Bernadette's authentic apparitions.

The upsurge in Marian visionaries—or those who claim to see Jesus on a nearly daily basis—is also a throwback to the beginning of our century, when the Western Hemisphere got caught up in the madness of Spiritualism.

I don't know if the majority are inspired by Heaven or

Hell, but I do know beyond reasonable question that many, including some very well-known ones, involve an intermingling of the subconscious mind as well, on some occasions, as infusion by deceptive spirits; and when there are signs of such intermingling, the messages are a major dilemma. Overall, it is best to believe, said Pope Urban VIII, because if an apparition turns out to be true, we will be glad we responded to Mary's call, while if it *isn't* true, we will receive graces as if it *were* true. It is best to believe first, for we will be rewarded for our faith, as long as we do not cling to a mystic once we know he is false, or succumb to obsession, antagonism, and cultishness.

Some are diabolical, and *very* deceptive. Satan knows Scripture and Church tradition better than any human, so it is not easy to spot him in their counterfeit "messages," nor in the phenomenon of miraculous photographs, which the devil can readily contrive, along with a temporary feeling of tranquility. They betray themselves only with time, and usually through the bad "fruits" of tension, dissension, confusion, obsession, rudeness, ego, inconsistency, exaggeration, bickering, and most importantly, by far most important, a lack of humility in the visionary. The fruits to be studied are not so much in the "messages" as in the personal lives of the visionaries.

There are seers who prophesy specific times or dates for disasters, while others indicate self-centeredness. There are those who channel, allowing the voices of "Jesus" and "Mary" to speak through their mouths or write with their hands—which is obviously very risky, terribly risky, if Jesus it is not. There are others who are sought after for counsel in the same way people seek after fortunetellers. They can look clean, wholesome, and intelligent, for they all say the Rosary or read Scripture, they can look meek and humble—until you dig below the surface.

"Many pretend to see Jesus and the Mother of God, and to understand their words, but they are in fact lying," warned the Virgin of Medjugorje. *"It is a very grave sin, and it is necessary to pray very much for them."*

I don't doubt that some of the proliferating visionaries are having pure experiences, but there is a tremendous *intermingling* of deceptive spirits, and I'm convinced they are diluting real warnings (the warnings from places such as Fatima, Akita, and Medjugorje) with hyped-up versions of coming punishments and jumping the gun as far as when such punishments will arrive—leaving the flock, as Marie Julie Jehenny prophesied, in diversion and confusion. In *Deuteronomy* (18:22), Moses tells us that "when a prophet speaks in the name of the Lord, if the thing does not happen or come to pass, that is the thing which the Lord has not spoken; the prophet has spoken it presumptuously." We have also come to the stage Christ warned about, when he said, "Then if anyone says to you, 'Look, here is the Christ!' or 'There!' do not believe it. For false christs and false prophets will arise and show great signs and wonders, so as to deceive, if possible, even the elect (*Matthew* 24:23-24)."

This agitation of the spirits, this terrific turbulence, which has caused division among Christians, speaks loudly of unusual times, highly unusual times, and like other forms of evil, serves to indicate that something will happen to put us in order if we don't do so ourselves. So too, does the phenomena seen in the skies at seemingly legitimate sites of apparition, such as Medjugorje, indicate a final stage of spiritual denouement. Signs in the sky are a benchmark of spiritual turbulence. The kind of phenomena reported from Bosnia-Hercegovina also brings to mind Christ's prophecy of the Great Tribulation when he mentions that *"stars will fall from Heaven, and the powers of the heavens will be shaken* (in *Matthew* 24:29)," or when the Lord says, *"I will show wonders in the heavens (Joel* 2:30)."

Like millions of others, I witnessed the "miracle of the sun" a number of times at Medjugorje, and if that isn't a sign of the times—that millions have taken part in the greatest supernatural episode of modern history, with the tacit approval of the Pope—I don't know what is. The sun suddenly seemed to leap far from its place and below it was an incredible colored striation unlike any colors I had ever seen associated with a sunset.

Really it was nothing like a sunset. The striations slashed across the sky, and there were colors above the sun, too.

It seemed to be moving. It shifted and spun.

It *pulsed*.

A white shield or disc moved in front so I could stare wide-eyed without so much as squinting.

I studied it, gawked at it for several minutes, watching as a flash of blue or scarlet would give way to a wholly different shade of red or blue.

Then the sun would flash back to a normal setting. I'd seen sunsets in Hawaii, Tanzania, and New Zealand. I'd seen sunsets in Arizona, Colorado, and California. But nothing remotely like this. When I looked away there were no sunspots in my eyes, though the sun was still at strength. Nor did it feel in any way like I was hurting or even straining my retinas.

When, during my 1989 trip, I shifted my eyes to the cross atop Mount Krizevac, which was to my left, I saw a huge pale pink aura surrounding the mountain, and inside that aura, around the cross, was a distinct light-green luminosity.

I stared at that too for several minutes, studying it, blinking, looking away, then back again, to make sure it wasn't just some kind of aftereffect of staring at the sun, or a stereoscopic visual illusion. There was no such aura on any surrounding hills, however, and lights seemed to spring from the mountain to the point where, mesmerized, I lost my way on the path.

Along with several other pilgrims. I also watched one night as a "star" began moving about in the night sky, zigzagging, flitting, then splitting into *three* stars—three separate stars—which turned blue, white, and red. We watched that for ten or 15 minutes with binoculars.

Another night, as I stood on the balcony of a bed-and-breakfast that was within sight of Saint James Church, where the apparitions were occurring, I looked up at the moon, which was very bright, and as I did it immediately began parting.

It looked like the moon was splitting in two!

At first I took this to be a case of simple double vision.

I shut my eyes, refocused, and still the moon began to part.

I shut my eyes and refocused. It kept doing the same

thing. Soon it had split into two equally big orbs, each looking like the original moon—two moons now, widely parted from each other!

If this wasn't a "lying wonder" (*2 Thessalonians* 2:9), it was a sign that Medjugorje had cosmological significance and isn't your standard apparitional episode. I called to a woman from Detroit named Rose, an elderly, gray-haired woman who walked with a limp, telling her to look up at the moon. "What do you see?" I asked, saying nothing else.

"Good Lord. Two moons!"

They were right over Saint James Church.

I focused on the orb to the right and in it was the clear image or etching of an old bearded man whose face filled the "moon." I described him to Rose but she couldn't see him. She suggested a saint or Jesus, but the man looked like neither to me. I was mesmerized by this bearded person whom I had never seen portrayed in any pictures or statues that I could recall.

A few moments later I turned my attention to the other "moon." In that orb I saw the clear profile of a veiled woman. I knew who *that* symbolized. It was similar to something I saw at Fatima on visiting there in 1989, and to what I had seen in the strange globular light over New York so many years before.

On subsequent visits I saw a number of other phenomena at Medjugorje, including a large luminous white "dove" (really a flapping light) that rose from between the spires of Saint James just after noon on August 15, 1990.

The light hovered, swept over the terrain, remained motionless for several minutes not far from where I was, and then blinked out.

CHAPTER 32

There Is Still Time

I saw similar manifestations during a three-week pilgrimage in the autumn of 1989, traveling alone 3,200 miles through Europe, from Fatima to Turin and Rome. When I visited a church not far from Medjugorje, in Tihaljina, I encountered two statues that reminded me of the faces in those two "moons." One, to the left, was of the veiled Virgin, and another, to the right, as in the right orb, was an unknown bearded man who turned out to be the prophet Elijah.

"Lo, I will send you Elijah, the prophet, before the day of the Lord comes, the great and terrible day," says *Malachi* 3:23-24, *"to turn the hearts of the fathers to their children, and the hearts of the children to their fathers, lest I come and strike the land with doom."*

It was the opinion of Cardinal Ratzinger that such signs, seen by millions of pilgrims, including thousands of priests who have visited Medjugorje, are "signs that point to the insufficiency of the cultures stamped by rationalism and positivism that dominate us." The Pope himself, in a discussion with Bishop Pio Ricardo Bello of Venezuela about the apparitions at a site known as Betania, called the outbreak of apparitions a "sign of the times," language Ratzinger has likewise used.

Our Lady was more explicit. *"My children, pray!"* she said at Medjugorje. *"The world has been drawn into a great whirlpool. It does not know what it is doing. It does not realize in what sense it is sinking. It needs your prayers so that I can pull it out of this danger.* (2/17/84). *Jesus prefers that you address yourselves directly to Him rather than through an intermediary. In the meantime, if you wish to give yourselves completely to God and if you wish that I be your protector, then confide to me all your intentions, your fasts, and your sacrifices, so that I can dispose of them according to the will of God* (9/4/82). *The best fast is on bread and water. Through fasting and prayer, one can stop wars, one can suspend the laws of nature* (7/21/82). *Advance against Satan by means of prayer* (8/8/85). *I call on each one of you to consciously decide for God and against Satan. I am your mother and, therefore, I want to lead you all to complete holiness. I want each one of you to be happy here on earth and to be with me in Heaven* (5/25/87). *Every family must pray family prayers and read the Bible* (2/14/85). *The peace of the world is in danger* (1981). *Satan is working hard in the world* (1/14/85). *I have come to call the world to conversion for the last time* (5/2/82). *I invite you. I need you. You are important* (June 1981). *Open your heart to the Holy Spirit. Especially during these days the Holy Spirit is working through you* (5/23/85). *Advance against Satan by means of prayer. Put on the armor of battle and with the rosary in your hand, defeat him!* (8/8/85)."

There is still time. Clearly, we are entering the final hour of that battle, before the Immaculate and Sacred Hearts triumph, and there is still time for us to cast Satan from our midst before God takes such action for us. When we look back at LaSalette, we see that it has taken nearly a century and a half—148 years—for the bulk of prophecies to reach fulfillment; and that at Fatima the warning of a second war materialized twenty years after the prediction. Our dear Lord's warnings are *conditional*. And His punishment can be lessened or avoided altogether, as at Nineveh. If, however, we do not help Heaven send the demons back into the pit, their number will be enough not only to continue our great oppression but eventually to provoke yet more horrible traumas. The little pre-signs will evolve into the outright warnings spoken about at Medjugorje, and then, if still we proceed with blindness, major turmoil. *"You cannot imagine what is going to happen nor what the Eternal Father will send to earth,"* Mary said on June 24, 1983, and we have been given glimpses of what that may be—the extreme of situations that could arise—through the messages of LaSalette, Akita, and Fatima.

"The society of men is on the eve of the most terrible scourges and of gravest events," said Our Lady of LaSalette. *"No one will be able to escape so many afflications together."* At the first blow of His thundering sword, said Mary in 1846, *"the mountains and all nature will tremble in terror, for the disorders and crimes of men have pierced the vault of the heavens.*

"The stars will lose their regular motion, the moon will only reflect a faint reddish glow. Water and fire will give the earth's globe convulsions, and terrible earthquakes will swallow up mountains and cities."

There would be a series of wars until the Last War. The fire of Heaven would fall.

The prospect of "fire" brings to mind the revelations of Mary to Sister Agnes Sasagawa at Akita, Japan, in 1973, where a statue of Mary, as Our Lady of All Nations, shed tears on 101 occasions. *"Many men in this world afflict the Lord,"* said the Virgin. *"I desire souls to console Him to soften the anger of the Heavenly Father. I wish, with my Son, for souls who will repair by their suffering and their poverty for the sinners and ingrates. In order that the world might know His anger, the Heavenly Father is preparing to inflict a great chastisement on all mankind. With my Son I have intervened so many times to appease the wrath of the Father. I have prevented the coming of calamities by offering Him the suffering of the Son on the Cross, His precious Blood, and the beloved souls who console Him by forming a cohort of victim souls. Prayer, penance, and courageous sacrifices can soften the Father's anger.*

"If men do not repent and better themselves, the Father will inflict a terrible punishment on all humanity. It will be a punishment greater than The Flood, such as one will

never have been seen before. Fire will fall from the sky and will wipe out a great part of humanity, the good as well as the bad, sparing neither priests nor faithful. The survivors will find themselves so desolate that they will envy the dead."

If such visions appear dire, it is because they are dire. But they represent, perhaps, extreme possibilities and not necessarily what will happen. With prayer and conversion they can be lessened or averted. Clearly, Cardinal Ratzinger had no problem with the warning issued from Akita, for he approved the pastoral letter from the local bishop, John Shorjiro Ito, endorsing Sister Agnes' message. There are those who go so far as to speculate that the Akita message bears similarities to the Third Secret of Fatima.

This was important to me because I have tried, as you may have noted, to quote only Church-approved apparitions, with a few exceptions like Medjugorje. It is also important because of the strength of the Akita message, which, if true, means we are indeed at risk of great chastisement.

The same foreboding came from Ecuador, where I purchased the reproduction of a miraculous image of Our Lady of Seven Sorrows, the one that resembled what I'd seen on Good Friday of 1984. When Our Lady, in that Church-approved apparition, appeared in Ecuador during 1634, she warned that the 19th and twentieth centuries would be a time of heresies and moral calamities, with just a faithful remnant left behind to combat *"the spirit of impurity which like a deluge of filth will flood the streets, squares, and public places."* Priestly vocations would be lost, nuns would leave their communities, and the faithful would endure unspeakable sufferings. Dark would descend on the Church, and Satan would gain control through faithless men, especially the wealthy who would become so selfish as to refuse financial aid to fight the rising evils.

"Satan will take control of this earth through the fault of faithless men who, like a black cloud, will darken the clear sky of the republic consecrated to the most Sacred Heart of my Divine Son. This republic, having allowed entry to all the vices, will have to undergo all sorts of chastisements: plagues, famine, war, apostasy, and the loss

of souls without number. And to scatter these black clouds blocking the brilliant dawning of the freedom of the Church, there will be terrible war in which the blood of priests and of religious will flow.

"That night will be so horrible that the wickedness will seem triumphant. Then will come my time: in astounding fashion I shall destroy Satan's pride, casting him beneath my feet, chaining him up in the depth of Hell, leaving Church and country freed at last from his cruel tyranny."

It would seem that the period for doubting apparitions has long since passed. There is simply too much documentation, too many facts to deny that God (or His messenger) is trying to reach His people in this rather sinful and deluded era. And it is equally undeniable that we are receiving some rather stern and pointed warnings of what our future might entail if we continue to turn our backs on our Creator.

But there is one other common thread in all of these messages, and it is common to the Bible as well. Perhaps it is the most important ingredient of all. And that is, God's Mercy!

He has always called His people to come back, to reform, prior to any purification required on His part. It is no different today. It is a common element with all of the mystics of this century. Somewhere in those messages is the request for us to recognize that God is forgiveness personified.

Pope John Paul II provided the world with official recognition of the Divine Mercy when he beatified Sr. Faustina on April 18, 1993. Sr. Faustina Kowalska, who died in 1938, was the beneficiary of some rather remarkable messages from Jesus Christ in the early part of this century. In the 1930s, prior to her death, she wrote of diary of some 600 pages recording the revelations of God's Mercy. She repeatedly mentions that Jesus had insistently told her that these are the times of His Divine Mercy, that this is the era of His Mercy, a period of grace and a turning away from evil. Sr. Faustina's memoirs are rife with extraordinary promises that Jesus reportedly stated were available to those souls who turned to His Mercy for their salvation and deliverance from the evils of this world.

In 1981, Pope John Paul II reaffirmed many of these graces in his published encyclical letter, *Rich In Mercy,* in which he speaks of Christ as the "incarnation of mercy... the inexhaustible source of mercy." The Pope went on to say, "at no time, especially at a moment as critical as our own, can the Church forget the prayer that is a cry for the mercy of God...The Church has the right and the duty to appeal to the God of Mercy 'with loud cries.'"

The Divine Mercy messages as recorded by Sr. Faustina state that Christ told her we must trust totally in His Love and Mercy: *"I am Love and Mercy itself... Let no soul fear to draw near to Me, even though its sins be scarlet...My mercy is greater than your sins and those of the entire world...I let my Sacred Heart be pierced with a lance, thus opening wide the source of mercy for you. Come then with trust to draw graces from this fountain...I never reject a contrite heart."* He also asked for special recognition of the hour that recalls His death on the cross, telling Sr. Faustina: *"At three o'clock, implore My mercy, especially for sinners; and, if only for a brief moment, immerse yourself in My Passion, particularly in My abandonment at the moment of agony. This is the hour of great mercy..."*

If we are to think in terms of any "final hour," we first need to think in terms of "the hour of great mercy."

CHAPTER 33

The Sign of Job

When I spoke to Father Jozo Zovko, the Croatian priest who'd been pastor at Medjugorje and also served at the church in Tihaljina, where I saw the statue of Elijah, he said our century is more evil than previous centuries but compared it not so much to the time of Nineveh as to the Book of *Job*. Satan is being allowed to test humanity, he said, all of humanity, and if we don't pass the test, then, I surmised, we can expect certain prophetic segments in *Isaiah, Daniel,* and *Revelation* to materialize.

"In this century Satan succeeded in having legalized something that is a terrible slaughter—abortion," said Father Jozo. "In this century America failed. And people have lost the sacred state of marriage, which is the very spring of life. Abortion is presenting the power of Satan, and man is in a time when prophets are necessary [see *Amos* 3:7]. To destroy the value of what is sacred is to shake the whole list of what is natural in human beings. It is the same as happened at the end of the Roman Empire—and that empire declined. And this world too cannot survive. It has turned to the tower of Babylon. It cannot stand. It will fall. It is like snow melting down, and it is all because man has accumulated illusions."

Father Jozo told me he has often encountered manifestations of the devil "in people who can become overcome

215

and possessed by Satan, who causes confusion and fear." He said he has seen "a countless number" of people who are afflicted by demons and that he realized it was a genuine phenomenon when the demons reacted to his prayers even if those prayers were said in a language unknown to the person afflicted.

When it comes to locutions and apparitions it is Jozo's feeling that we shouldn't be surprised that the Lord is trying to communicate often, "for He is the Word."

But neither should we be diverted from the Bible by becoming too preoccupied with private revelations. "I am looking at these things in a simple way. I read the Gospels. I don't feel the need to think about (chastisements). I think about *today*. I am the kind of man who says whatever happens is God's will."

The warnings contained in secrets such as those dispensed at LaSalette and Medjugorje should neither consume nor divert us from the key message of prayer, fasting, and hope.

But Father Jozo added: "It is going to be interesting to watch what happens after these secrets, because many will say, 'Why didn't these children tell us so we could have changed?' "

In February of 1993 I trekked for a third time to Medjugorje to pray for discernment. I did so knowing Pope John Paul II has, on several occasions, expressed informal approval of the apparitions. ("Yes, it's good for pilgrims to go to Medjugorje and pray and do penance," the Pope reportedly said during a meeting with Bishop Silvester Treinen of Boise in 1989, adding to a group of pro-life physicians later that same year, "Today's world has lost its sense of the supernatural. But many are searching for it—and find it in Medjugorje through prayer, fasting, and penance.") John Paul was especially aware that a prophecy concerning his native Poland—a prophecy to the effect that the just would prevail there—had already proven itself when Lech Walesa took the reigns of government from the Communists.

But John Paul also knew that the world's situation remained precarious, and that precariousness was expressed most powerfully in what was happening right there in Bosnia-Hercegovina. This region where Mary had first come 12 years before—as "Queen of Peace," warning Yugoslavians and the world that *the peace of the world is in danger*—was now engulfed in horrible tribal and religious fighting, the worst war on European soil since World War II, in the words of Secretary of State Warren Christopher himself, "a war from Hell." I visited cathedrals in Mostar which had been utterly destroyed by the Serbians, and I listened at night to the echo of mortars.

Sarajevo is not far from Medjugorje, and it was in besieged Sarajevo, as I recall, that Mirjana had an apparition of the devil.

The road sign pointing to Medjugorje was riddled with bullets and at the home of visionary Ivanka Elez, windows were taped so as not to shatter from the reverberations of distant shells as Satan unleashed a torrent against the Virgin, closing Medjugorje to the world and trying to instigate the Third World War.

By 1993 four of the visionaries had been given nine secrets while the other two seers, Ivanka and Mirjana, possessed all ten. They didn't know each other's secrets. They didn't know how many were the same. They were concerned only with their own. Some of the messages were personal, some pertained to the Church, others concerned Medjugorje and the world. We know only that the first three secrets granted to Mirjana, the first visionary to receive all ten, involve events that will come as warnings to all mankind, along with a great sign or miracle. In his 1983 report to the Pope, Father Tomislav Vlasic said that "after the visible sign, those who are still alive will have little time for conversion. For that reason, the Blessed Virgin calls for urgent conversion and reconciliation. The invitation to prayer and penance is destined to ward off evil and war and above all to save souls. . . After the admonitions, the visible sign will appear on the site of the apparitions in Medjugorje for all the world to see. The sign will be given as a testimony to the apparitions and in order to call people back to faith."

No one knew much about Mirjana's fourth, fifth, and sixth secrets, but, as Father Vlasic points out, "The ninth and tenth secrets are serious. They concern chastisement for the sins of the world. Punishment is inevitable, for we cannot expect the whole world to be converted. *The punishment can be diminished by prayer and penance* (my emphasis), but it cannot be eliminated. Mirjana says that one of the evils that threatened the world, the one contained in the seventh secret, has been averted thanks to prayer and fasting. That is why the Blessed Virgin continues to encourage prayer and fasting: 'You have forgotten that through prayer and fasting you can avert war and suspend the laws of nature.'

"After the first admonition, the others will follow in a rather short time. Thus, people will have some time for conversion.

"That interval will be a period of grace and conversion."

While a great evil threatening mankind and contained in the seventh secret has been eliminated or lessened, the last three secrets, it appears, still await humankind. "The eighth secret is worse than the seven before it," said Mirjana. "I begged for it to be made less severe. Every day I beseeched the Madonna to get it mitigated, and at last she said that if everyone prayed it might be averted. But then she told me the ninth secret, and it was even worse. As for the tenth, it is terrible, and nothing can alter it. It will happen."

In 1992 I obtained the tape of an interview conducted by Father Peter Ljubicic with Mirjana, who had chosen him as a spiritual director. In the interview with Ljubicic, Mirjana used much stronger language than she does with pilgrims or journalists. She was most concerned about mankind doing "penance and sacrifices, especially now before the first secret. If you knew how it gets to me when I think about it! If Our Lady wasn't with me I would probably go crazy, knowing what is waiting for us. The young people don't know what's awaiting them. I cry and pray for them and ask Our Lady to enlighten them." She went on, "The world has never been like this. God has never been prayed to less than this time. Everything is more important than God. That's why she is crying. I'm sorry for the people because they don't know what they're headed for. If they could look into the secrets, how they are, they would change right away."

When I interviewed Mirjana I learned that the current war in Bosnia-Hercegovina, the war within earshot of Medjugorje itself, is *not* part of her secrets. The first secret is yet to come and it is "nothing good," more severe than some of the other secrets, an event that will be sent "to shake us up so the world will start thinking." Yet she added that it is "not a catastrophe in a huge sense, but to prove there is God." She said our scientists will try to explain events in the first two secrets as natural phenomena, and that the first secret will be directly seen not by the entire world but only by those in the locality or region where it occurs.

When asked if it would take place in Medjugorje she declined to comment.

Most interesting is what Mirjana replied when asked if people would rush to wherever the event contained in the secret occurs. "Father," said Mirjana, "no one would want to go and see the kind of event that will take place. For example, people would not want to go to Italy to see how a dam collapsed."

There will be periods of grace between secrets, but those periods, she told Ljubicic, could be very short. One secret could unfold today, and another tomorrow. Right now we are in a period of grace during which Heaven is trying to transform our lives, such that we avert massive destruction.

At the onset or fulfillment of the secrets, says Mirjana and the other seers, Satan's extended power, his special influence, will be broken.

"When the sign appears, no one will any longer doubt that God truly exists," said Mirjana. "But it will be too late for many to convert. The encounter with Divine reality will be catastrophic for those who have not already turned toward God. But for those who have done so, it will be a time of great joy."

A third visionary, Marija Pavlovic, who also had a secret pertaining to the sign (one secret we know they share), said that "this is a time of great grace and mercy. Now is the time to listen to these messages and to change our lives. Those who do so will never be able to thank God enough."

How the world will be changed we don't know, but afterward, said Father Vlasic, we will believe and worship as

in ancient times. It is my personal conclusion that the
visionaries may know a little less than what many people
have assumed, and that while they have been given premo-
nitions and insights into certain specific events, they cannot necessarily see the whole mosaic of our hereafter. They
have been given bits and pieces—far more than the rest of
us, but no key to the entire unfolding of the future. Certain
aspects of coming occurrences have been shown them in
closeup, and thus the fright, as one might expect fright at
a magnified look at soldiers blowing up a dam, for example, with floodwaters rushing into a home the seers might
have been shown in vision; it would be a terrible sight but
not necessarily a mega-event. That neither Mirjana nor two
other visionaries I spoke with, Jacov and Vicka, seem to
have been forewarned of the specific hostilities now surrounding Medjugorje confirmed that God allows no one
person knowledge of His entire plan.

"Our Lady says this is a time of great grace," said Vicka.
"She is here to convert us at this moment. She says this
is a serious moment. Our Lady says each one of us is going
to have to account for our sins. She doesn't want to lose
any of her children. She didn't say anything about
'cataclysms' that will come. Our Lady does not want to
scare us. There are secrets that are good and bad. Our Lady
is giving us the strength to accept these secrets. In this
moment Satan is very strong and wants to destroy marriages, youth, and peace. Our Lady has said this before and
is saying it again in these times. It is a time of special
power for Satan."

When I asked if this century had been given to Satan,
Vicka replied, "Our Lady didn't say yesterday, today, or
tomorrow. She said 'these times,' not 'this century.'"
So too did Mirjana back away from earlier remarks about
a specific time period. "Satan is very strong this century.
Our Lady didn't say anything about the period that belongs
to Satan. Our Lady said we have to pray because Satan is
very strong. By your prayers the power of Satan will be
less. When we started to pray at Medjugorje his power
started to become less, and that's why he has become
aggressive. Once Our Lady said, 'Wherever I go, Satan is

following me. He cannot stand to see people praying.' I think Satan is as strong as we give him.''

Jacov added, "In the messages of Our Lady we can see Our Lady has talked much about Satan, that he wants to destroy our lives and he has his own plans like Our Lady.''

It was interesting to me that the visionaries had built new homes, and Mirjana told me she expects to have occasional apparitions of Our Lady through the rest of her life (or so it came through in interpretation). Jacov showed mild disdain for the many visionaries elsewhere who had predicted specific catastrophes which never came to be. "I was reading in a newsletter that we are in the face of catastrophes, and if it is true, we should be in that catastrophe at this moment," he commented. "We do not have to think of catastrophes.''

When I asked about the flurry of other apparitionists around the world, especially in the United States, Vicka said, "Our Lady didn't say they're true or not. We asked her but she didn't give us an answer. We don't receive an answer. She is quiet.''

So too was Mary quiet about precise time frames. But I know this much: the upheaval in Yugoslavia began about ten years after she first appeared in Medjugorje, and I wondered if the other nations where Mary is supposed to be appearing—Ukraine, Ireland, Italy, the U.S.—would suffer similar stress commencing about ten years after apparitions erupted in those places. This is just a question. I know that with the Lord an "hour" can be decades, and many or even most of us may never live to see the denouement.

But was the mayhem in Bosnia and Croatia a pre-sign of armed conflict elsewhere in the world, such as China, Korea, or the U.S.S.R., just as tremblers might be a pre-sign of geophysical disturbances?

Was not former Yugoslavia a microcosm of the former republics of the Soviet Union?

"Satan is strong and wants to destroy and deceive you in many ways," said Our Lady on September 25, 1990. *"I call you, dear children, to grasp the importance of my coming and the seriousness of the situation* (8/25/91). *For now as never before Satan wants to show the world his shameful*

face by which he wants to seduce as many people as possible on to the way of death and sin (9/25/91). *Satan wants war."*

On June 25, 1993, Ivanka received her annual apparition, and according to one witness, the seer, who no longer experiences daily visitations, was in the presence of Our Lady for about ten minutes. Afterward, overwhelmed, Ivanka broke down and cried. Apparently she was shown previews of events that may happen if mankind does not pray and convert. While some might consider Ivanka's apparition "gloom and doom," it jived with a message given that same day to the seer Marija, who receives the monthly message to the world and who reported that the Virgin said we are in "special" times during which she is attempting "to protect your hearts from Satan." The events Ivanka was shown are not necessarily part of her secrets and did not pertain solely to former Yugoslavia but to "the whole of humanity."

"I saw awful, horrible pictures, and Our Lady was crying so much," said Ivanka. "Simply she is inviting all of us to open our hearts so her Son can take us by the hand and lead us onto the right path. This is most important. She blessed all of us and just said, 'pray, pray, pray.'"

CHAPTER 34

The Heavenly Gaze

It was my speculation, after reviewing hundreds of heavenly messages, as well as the general and startling state of the world, that the coming times could shape up something like this:

We might see, in the next few years, a further escalation of societal evil, especially in the form of coldness, violence, and immorality. As we continue into the spiritual chastisement, we could continue to experience an increase in personal difficulties, including individual spiritual harassment as Satan lashes out especially at those who have joined the legion of Christ and Mary. We probably will be haunted by more spiritual agitation in the Church (which is on the brink of purification) and by more confusion in the form of false prophecy. More than anything we will see efforts by Satan at spiritual division.

In an attempt to nudge us into realization, hopefully God will send more little hints in the way of both miracles and regional events. There may be additional peculiarities in the weather, and certain parts of the world may experience acute political or geophysical disturbances. These disturbances could slowly increase in intensity and erupt into major, perhaps even unprecedented, events if we do not respond to previous hints, such as the Mississippi flood. The important word here is "if." *If* mankind persists in its debauchery there may come an event that frightens all of us back to our senses. Such an event or events may arrive during the next several decades. They could occur during the first half of the next century or they could occur, if many mystics are to be believed, during the last part of this decade. I feel they will occur between now and around the year 2040.

I believe that the intervention of Mary at places such as Medjugorje, and the intercessory prayers of many millions responding to her call, have already postponed certain trends leading into the steeper curve of chastisement. I also believe that the continuation of this postponement hinges upon a decision or series of decisions that will soon confront all of society. We will be presented during the next few years with a new challenge. We will soon be given a choice of whether to accept a new evil or reject it as the work of Satan. This evil will appear to have beneficial effects but like nothing else will—if we accept it—lead us quickly into unpleasant circumstances. I have no way of knowing what it is but have wondered if it might be something like acceptance of euthanasia or the abortion pill RU-486.

At some point in the not too distant future—again, during the next several decades—I believe we may experience not the formal Second Coming but a major manifestation of Christ, Who will come in a manner similar to how His mother has come at Medjugorje. He will come in light and on a cloud. It will be believed by some and ridiculed by others.

Such a manifestation will mark the change of era. We will be at the end of Satan's era and into the triumph (as promised at Fatima) of Mary's Immaculate Heart. Although it may not look like it now, and although I have been given the trying task, in the book you've just read, of detailing a long litany of evil, we are on the verge of an assured victory. Mary is going to win. She will not be defeated by the Red Dragon. That has never been the question. The question is how much agony humankind will put itself through before coming to its collective senses and purging Satan from its midst. The question is how much damage Satan will be able to inflict before the triumph of Mary and the manifestations of Jesus bring an end to Lucifer's extended power.

Whether or not we are in the so-called End Times, we are in stages described in the Book of Revelation. And as Father Jozo said, we are all Job. It's a highly unusual time, and the best part is that we are going to win. Satan is soon to be vanquished. God will get through to us. He is not out to scare us but to lead us into purification. The war is going to be won in a way that will amaze many people. It is going to be won by a unification of Christians and by simple prayer. We are going to learn how very powerful prayer can be, especially, in the Catholic domain, the prayer of Mass.

This is the greatest weapon of war, the Holy Sacrifice. At Medjugorje Mary tells us that the Mass is so powerful we can never understand just how powerful it is while we are still of earthly minds. Christ is truly present in the Eucharist, and when we receive Him the attacks by Satan lose their power. I have seen this time and again, how Communion removes confusion and settles the spirit. It is *extremely* important. And the fact that Christ is manifest in the Eucharist is indicated to us through the many miracles in which the Host has transformed or shed blood.

Those of us who are Catholics must immerse ourselves in the Mass, knowing without doubt that a single person participating with true strength and faith can break down a towering evil stronghold. A single person, working with Christ, and without fear, can help break down a principality.

Taking our concerns and lifting them from our hearts during Consecration will effect enormous change.

Whether Catholic or non-Catholic, we must go back to the Bible. We must digest the New Testament. We must read it every day. How many times did I myself see evil assaults disappear—VANISH!—after a reading of biblical passages? The Bible remains the key. At times of personal attack I found it especially comforting to read *Ephesians* or *Psalms*.

Leaving an open Bible in the house dissuades evil spirits, as does holy water and blessed salt.

Plead the Blood of Jesus. Plead His Mercy over every

aspect of your lives. Plead the Blood which sends demons to flight.

When Satan disrupts our lives, sending us anxious or confused thoughts, we must immediately halt what we are doing and pray until the evil attack is stopped. We must pray until peace returns to our spirits. We must nip his obnoxious diversions in the bud.

He sends many people—good and bad—our way. He can use the holy as well as the sinful. He is relentless, but when we approach his attempts with humility and peace of heart, we stifle him.

He is afraid of humility.

And he flees the Holy Spirit, who especially comes when we praise Jesus and thank the Eternal Father over and over.

He flees when we thank and love God.

We must move together. We must expand the collective recitation of the Rosary and charismatic prayer. We must spend yet more time in front of the Blessed Sacrament. And we must do so specifically petitioning Heaven to expose the evil and wipe it away with His Light.

We must pray that society comes out of its current state of blindness and denial.

There are some who misuse the term "gloom and doom." It is not gloom and doom to expose evil. The true gloom is to continue wallowing in Satan's work. To pretend matters are better than they are is to conveniently disregard the work we must hurriedly tend to. Evil is far more pervasive than what most people want to believe. To expose it is to move toward a remedy. I saw this at Love Canal, when everyone said writing about toxic chemicals was "doom and gloom" but the result was a national effort at cleaning up toxic dumps that (as it turns out) threatened many thousands of Americans.

Specific prayer aimed at opening society's eyes will go a long way toward exposing evil, and I believe that praying in unison will indeed bring mankind to its senses before any truly global disaster.

Invoking the saints and angels is extremely powerful. They come when they are called. They respond to our needs. They help fix our eyes in a heavenly gaze.

And that's what is needed most: the heavenly gaze. We

must note the evil but not become obsessed with it. Once we know the enemy we look up to God and His angels for spiritual support.

Come ye angels of Heaven! Surround us this very moment! Come in throngs and hordes. Come by the millions!

We look up—we keep our eyes focused on Heaven—at the same time we do what the figure in my dream once said. When evil rises in our lives, our families, or society at large, when we see it as New Age or immorality, when the demons come to harass in their final pathetic assault, we remain in a heavenly gaze while lifting up our collective hand and commanding the devil in the name of Jesus to vanish.

CHAPTER 35

The Prayers of Faith and Love

So it is that we stand with Christ and our Blessed Mother on the cosmic battlefield, knowing that a bright era will follow the darkness. But knowing too that the battle has not yet reached its height. *"I tell you again, do not live in fear of the devil's evils,"* said a message to one of the North American visionaries who I felt was worthy of official scrutiny. *"Instead, look at them, look at them well! Tear off the malefactor's numerous masks and firmly confront him. Let the gifts of My Spirit be your shield. Make your sincere, living prayer your weapon."*

Most powerful are the prayers of faith, love, and suffering. The devil always flees when rebuked by those soft of heart. He flees from humbleness. He flees especially from the powerful prayers of the suffering. He flees from the prayers of those in wheelchairs, or those battling cancer. He flees from those who offer up their depression or mourning. He flees from those who offer up their suffering asking nothing in return. God lessens chastisement when we suffer for purification, just as He responded when the residents of Nineveh donned sackcloth. As one mystical revelation said, "A faithful soul is more powerful than Hell, but a crucified soul is more powerful than a thousand hells."

228

It is through those battles, those times of pain and loneliness, those times of suffering, and fasting, that we are strengthened and draw nearer to Him. At Fatima Jacinta and Francisco had suffered greatly and offered up that intense suffering—at such a young age—for the salvation of "poor sinners." In tender youth Jacinta and Francisco had understood the tremendous power of suffering. They learned, as did so many saints, to welcome and embrace suffering, to savor it. They had died of influenza before they were teenagers.

"Do you suffer much?" Lucia once asked Francisco at his sickbed.

"Bastante," replied the infirm boy. "But it doesn't matter. I suffer to console Our Lord, and in a little while I shall be with Him."

Right there is the main message of what God has sent in the way of supernatural communication since the days of Job and especially since Jesus. Life is a trial. It is not the end of the road. It is the testing grounds. It's an obstacle course. When we rise above bitterness and suffering—which are given to everyone in various forms—we work our way closest to eternal happiness.

Those who suffer and fast not only serve as our best prayer-warriors but also lessen for themselves their stay in Purgatory. We are told by the mystics that every moment on earth, every moment in the struggle down here, is worth days, months, years, or even centuries of Purgatory, when we suffer prayerfully. This is a vital lesson, for according to the visionaries, Purgatory can be an awful place, with many different levels. At the lowest region is a fire like hellfire, with terrible heat or cold, or chambers of suffering that are like being in a terrifically cold, dank cell full of miserable clinging sand and unable to move. Higher levels, according to Medjugorje, are like a rainy or murky day, with souls weeping in the fog for they now know eternity exists, and they suffer the terrible absence of not being able, for the time being, while they are in the process of purification, of seeing God. We must thus also pray each day not only to lessen our own Purgatory but for those poor souls who suffer there now, thirsting for our every *Our*

Father or *Hail Mary,* which brings refreshment as does water to a soul lost in the desert.

"When I was shown Purgatory, I couldn't see anything," Vicka told me. "It is dark like ash. You can hear people moaning and trembling. You can hear there is someone but you cannot see."

On July 21, 1982, the visionaries were told, *"There are many souls in Purgatory. There are also persons who have been consecrated to God—some priests, some religious. Pray for their intentions, at least the* Lord's Prayer, *the* Hail Mary, *and the* Glory Be, *seven times each, and the* Creed. *I recommend it to you. There is a large number of souls who have been in Purgatory for a long time because no one prays for them."*

At Medjugorje it was also said that *"in Purgatory there are different levels. The lowest is close to Hell, and the highest gradually draws near to Heaven. It is not on All Soul's Day but at Christmas that the greatest number of souls leave Purgatory. In Purgatory there are souls who pray ardently to God, but for whom no relative or friend prays on earth. God makes them benefit from the prayers of other people. It happens that God permits them to manifest themselves in different ways, close to their relatives on earth, in order to remind men of the existence of Purgatory and to solicit their prayers to come close to God Who is just but good. The majority of people go to Purgatory. Many go to Hell. A small number go directly to Heaven."*

Fasting helps us approach Heaven and ward off evil attacks. There are few things which are more powerful against Satan. It was no coincidence that Jesus fasted for forty days before publicly entering the spiritual combat. With fasting we are made stronger and purified. It breaks demonic bondages and sets us free from past dabblings in the occult, wrongful sexual dalliances, and other transgressions. We need to learn how to pray and suffer, when suffering we are called to endure, for through suffering, which we all encounter in life, we are given an opportunity to defeat Satan and draw sweetness from discomfort, as well as lessen our stay in Purgatory. Life is a trial. Life is suffering. Life is a period of probation. Once we acknowledge that fact we transcend it. Life is one big trial in which we choose for or against God.

Every moment on earth is crucial, full of tests and tribulations. Life is suffering, and when we do it well, when we don't complain, when we rise above its snares, when we are not made bitter, it turns into the greatest of grace.

"Do not let Satan block you on the way," said Mary at Medjugorje. *"Dear children, pray and accept all that God is offering you on this way which is bitter, but to whomever is engaged in it, God reveals joy and sweetness to respond in good heart to His calls."*

"Pray," she pled, *"that every trial of Satan be transformed to the glory of God."*

I recall one morning, an early morning, walking back from the small dark church below Assisi, the church of San Damiano. I was walking past an olive grove when something told me to pick one of the olives and taste it. They were on the branches overhanging the walk. I knew the olives weren't ripe—they were small and light green—but I plucked one anyway and bit into it.

Instantly my mouth was filled with the strongest, most awful bitterness I had ever encountered. It was terrible. It was a taste I'll never forget, so sour it actually caused suffering.

But I kept up my prayer without disturbance of heart, and as I approached the Basilica of Saint Francis, an incredible thing happened. Suddenly the bitterness was gone and there was an impossible aftertaste—a beautiful delectable aftertaste. The very thing which had caused bitterness had now evolved into a sweetness filling my mouth. I'll never forget it. I can't come close to describing its pleasure. It was the most delicious taste I had ever experienced, and where the bitterness had lasted a few minutes, the sweetness lasted for several hours.

Then there is the prayer of faith, with which we soundly defeat the harassing presence of demons. We must never fear devils, for to do so is to express a faith in Lucifer's power and a *lack* of faith in the power of Almighty God. "I am quite sure I am more afraid of people who are themselves terrified of the devil than I am of the devil himself," said Saint Teresa. "'Oh, the devil, the devil!' we say, when we might be saying 'God! God!' and making the devil tremble."

The devil delights in our fear, feeding off it, while fleeing when we despise or ridicule him. *"Apri la bocca metteti caco!"* was what Saint Francis instructed his disciples to tell the demon. He tries to intimidate us, but he doesn't win unless we let him. In 1988, when I was arranging to send my mother to Medjugorje, there was a serious fire in my house, and I lost my clothes, my computer, my holy pictures, tape recorders, and just about everything I owned. I learned to laugh at this harassment. Afterward, I ended up with more than I ever had before. With a Rosary, evil is quickly dispelled, and also by spending time in front of the Blessed Sacrament.

When we have faith in God we rise above the storm clouds, we transcend the maelstrom, instead of looking up at the clouds and listening fretfully to the echoes of thunder, with our feet mired in the mud. When we have faith, the proper level of faith, the faith that maintains itself beyond little disappointments, beyond the trials that seek to *rob* us of that faith, we become one with the power of Eternity. We are powerful when we invoke the angels like Michael, whose presence I felt upon visiting the cave dedicated to him on Monte San Angelo in Italy.

I remember a little example of faith, a tiny example, during that 1991 trip, when I was researching *The Final Hour.* I was driving across Italy in the middle of the night, because I wanted to spend Sunday at Monte San Angelo as well as nearby San Giovanni Rotundo, where Padre Pio is buried.

I felt full of faith that night, and I needed it because I knew I would not arrive at San Giovanni Rotundo until three or four in the morning, and at such an hour there would likely be no hotel rooms in that small and backward town. I prayed. I prayed for a hotel room, knowing the hotels already would be filled with weekend pilgrims. I prayed to make up $25, because that day I had overspent by such an amount and was on a tight budget. I prayed especially that I would somehow find a place to Xerox my notebook and send a copy back to the United States, because I planned, after visiting San Giovanni Rotundo, to catch a ferry to Croatia, which was under attack by the Serbs and thus presented me with the specter of having my notes confiscated and losing all the valuable research.

I prayed to find a Xerox center knowing there were none in San Giovanni Rotundo on a Sunday.

As expected, when I got to San Giovanni there were no rooms. The hotels were full. I knocked on every one of them, and by the time I got to the last inn, I began wondering if I was going to have to sleep in my car. It was the last possible hotel. But still I had faith, and at the last place, a night clerk came out, rubbed his eyes (he had been sleeping), and told me he had room for two others who had also come but not for me.

However, he looked at me and a thought struck him. "I am not going back to sleep, so you can have the room we use to sleep in, the night clerk's room," he said in broken English. "It is not a real hotel room, it has no bathroom, so I will let you have it for $25 less than normal."

I remember trudging in exhaustion down the hall, putting my key in the door, and opening it only to see not just a desperately needed bed but also a Xerox machine.

Faith. Faith and vigilance. When we realize evil for what it is—when we recognize where an anxious or foul thought comes from—we're better able to deal with it, and the way we deal with it is by blunting it with faith and love of God.

With love of God we are shielded. With faith we fly above demonic attack. I'm the last person to underestimate the devil's power, but no matter how powerful he seems, his force is less than the power of angels like Michael, and it cannot possibly stand up to the Blood of Christ.

We win with faith, and with faith we shall defeat evil and lessen the purifications and chastisements. To do this we need to consecrate ourselves.

"O Immaculate Heart of Mary, overflowing with goodness, show us your love for us. May the flame of your heart, Oh Mary, descend upon all peoples. We love you immensely. Impress in our hearts a true love. Through your most sacred and maternal heart, to which we consecrate our-

selves, cure us from every spiritual illness, and make us capable of looking at the beauty of your eternal heart."

The Virgin purifies our requests and augments them. She is our mother. She is the light in the darkness. She has told us time and again that her Immaculate Heart will win—as it will—but that we need to help her, we need to prove ourselves in battle, and we need also to consecrate ourselves to her Son's Sacred Heart.

"O Jesus, we know that You are sweet. That You have given Your Heart for us. It was crowned with thorns by our sins. Save us and everyone we know from the fires of Hell and Purgatory. Through Your most Sacred Heart, make us all love one another. Cause hatred to disappear among mankind. Show us Your Love. All of us love You. And we desire that You protect us with Your Heart of the Good Shepherd. Enter into each heart, Jesus! Knock on the door of our hearts. Be patient and tenacious with us. We are still locked up in ourselves, because we have not understood Your Will. Knock continuously, Oh Jesus. Make our hearts open to You, at least in reminding us of the Passion which You suffered for us. Free us from every evil and hatred!"

That is the final prayer of the warrior: love. There is nothing more powerful. Love has dominance over every evil and hatred. We love when we work at longsuffering, patience, tolerance, kindness, humility, and forgiveness. Humility is the bridge to Heaven and love is the wood. We win the war when we work at loving every single person we see in the course of a day, every friend, every stranger, no matter how much they irritate us. We win when we avoid pride, envy and jealousy, which are subtle forms of hatred.

Pride is the greatest enemy.

We must reconcile ourselves with each other, and with other religious faiths. There must be no division. We must find common ground. Forget the petty differences. We all face a common enemy and he is making his final offensive. We are called in this life to defeat demons, overwhelm them with our faith and unity, and come to the rescue of our hell-bent society. "The Virgin Mary always stressed that there is but one God, and that people have caused the divisions," Mirjana told Father Vlasic in 1983, many years before ethnic fighting broke out in Bosnia. "One cannot truly believe, be a true Christian, if he does not respect other religions as well."

"I invite you all to awaken your hearts to love," said Our Mother on April 25, 1993. *"Go into nature and look how nature is awakening, and it will be a help for you to open your hearts to the love of God, the Creator. I desire you to awaken love in your families, so that where there is unrest and hatred, love will reign, and when there is love in your hearts then there is also prayer. And, dear children, do not forget that I am with you and I am helping you with my prayer that God may give you the strength of love."*

We choose for God when we undertake voluntary penance in the form of fasting and loving our enemies. Through prayer and self-deprivation—taming the flesh—we still have the chance, Mary has told us at LaSalette, Fatima, Akita, Betania, and Medjugorje, of suspending or lessening future purification at both the personal and societal levels. We still have the chance, a good chance, of avoiding the fate of those who didn't listen to Noah.

We have a chance if we love. For when we love, we have access to God's greatest protection. We have access to His succor when, first and foremost, we love *Him.* We must pray for that love. We must praise and thank Him for His Love. Those of us who are Catholic can best do so at Holy Mass.

"Mass is the greatest prayer of God," says the Virgin. *"You will never be able to understand its greatness. That is why you must be perfect and humble at Mass, and you should prepare yourselves for it."*

When we tend to proper prayer, and when we truly love, we become healthier and more beautiful. When we love, our prayers are far more powerful. When we love, we are on the path away from Satan and toward the glory of joyful Eternity. Along with the descriptions of Purgatory and Hell, visionaries have also been given glimpses of Heaven. They are extraordinary images, of another world that is the true world, so much more alive and full of wonder than our own, with spectacular flows of living water and entirely spectacular refractions of light. It is a place where we see each other as spirits, no longer burdened by our physical bodies, and in communication with those we have known who have died before us. Everyone there is busy with joy. As it says in *1 Corinthians* 2:9, "Eye has not seen, ear has not heard, nor has it so much as dawned on man what God has prepared for those who love Him." They say that it's a place of incredible peace and happiness, with colors unlike any colors on earth, nearly crystalline, and songs different than anything earthlings could compose. "I saw these people as in a park," Mirjana told me. "And they were dressed like in the time when Jesus was on earth. You could see by their faces that they had the same peace. You can see that these faces have everything."

They have everything because they are finally able to see and praise the Living God, He Who formed us, He Who watches us every moment, He Who has put up with so much from us for so long; He Who wants us to be with Him forever and Who is vastly more powerful—infinitely more powerful—than the fallen angels.

That is what we have to look forward to: Heaven and God. The afterlife does exist. It is an actual reality that we must keep in mind every waking moment, strive for, pray for, fast for.

And we must love. For Heaven is love. God is Love. The light visionaries see upon entrance to Heaven is the light of love, and whether we are allowed *into* that light, at the moment of judgment, will depend, more than anything, more than any ritual or prayers, more even than suffering, on how often and much we have loved our fellow humans and most importantly how much we have loved and fought for the Eternal God.

"So humble yourselves under the mighty hand of God, that He may exalt you in due time. Cast all your worries upon Him because He cares for you.

"Be sober and vigilant. Your opponent the devil is prowling around like a roaring lion looking for someone to devour. Resist him, steadfast in faith, knowing that your fellow believers throughout the world undergo the same sufferings."

(2 Peter 5:6-9)

OTHER TITLES
by Michael H. Brown

THE FINAL HOUR
by Michael H. Brown

A summation of the reported apparitions of the Blessed Virgin Mary from around the world during the past 100 years. Investigative journalist Michael Brown, provides compelling information about our extraordinary era.

371 pages   **$11.50**

Josyp Terelya WITNESS
Autobiography by Josyp Terelya
Co-authored by Michael H. Brown

A dynamic autobiography. The story of a mystic, a visionary, a suffering servant, a victim of Communism, a leader in the underground Church in the Soviet Union.

344 pages   **$10.00**

Faith Publishing Company

Faith Publishing Company has been organized as a service for the publishing and distribution of materials that reflect Christian values, and in particular the teachings of the Catholic Church.

It is dedicated to publication of only those materials that reflect such values.

Faith Publishing Company also publishes books for The Riehle Foundation. The Foundation is a non-profit, tax-exempt producer and distributor of Catholic books and materials worldwide, and also supplies hospital and prison ministries, churches and mission organizations.

For more information on the publications of Faith Publishing Company, contact:

Faith Publishing Company
P.O. BOX 237
MILFORD, OHIO 45150

ADDITIONAL BOOKS FROM
Faith Publishing Company

SPIRITUAL WARFARE
by **Rev. George W. Kosicki, C.S.B.**

Some straight-forward facts about the existence of Satan, and his all-out-warfare being waged against this age, supported by biblical passages.

146 pages   **$5.00**

THE PAIN AND THE JOY
by **Fr. Edward Carter, S.J.**

By focusing on Christ's example we can live successfully Christian lives and survive against an onslaught of discouragement. Fr. Carter provides inspiring reflections revealing Jesus' answers to life's frustrations.

144 pages   **$5.00**

PRIMER OF PRAYER
by **Fr. Bartholomew J. O'Brien**

Provides the basics on prayer and progresses to address the different types of prayer: vocal, spontaneous, meditative and contemplative.

124 pages   **$3.00**

ADDITIONAL BOOKS FROM
Faith Publishing Company

APOCALYPSE
THE BOOK FOR OUR TIMES
by Fr. Albert J. Shamon

One of the best explanations of the symbolism of the Book of Revelation, and how Fr. Shamon relates Revelation to our own times, our own century, our own existence.

96 pages   **$4.00**

AN APPEAL FROM
MARY IN ARGENTINA
by Fr. René Laurentin

The incredible story of apparitions currently taking place in San Nicolás, Argentina, where the seer has received the stigmata. Mary's messages are preparing the world for the return of her Son, Jesus—calling people to open their hearts to His love and peace.

160 pages   **$6.00**

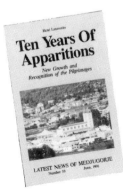

TEN YEARS OF
APPARITIONS
by Fr. René Laurentin

The events of Medjugorje from June 1990 thru June 1991. Interviews with the seers, analysis by Fr. Orec on the status of Medjugorje, and a last look at the country just prior to the war.

168 pages   **$6.00**

Books published by
Faith Publishing Company
can be ordered as follows:

Individuals send
requests to:

The Riehle Foundation
P.O. Box 7
Milford, Ohio 45150
513-576-0032

Book stores and
centers, contact:

Faith Publishing Company
P.O. Box 237
Milford, Ohio 45150
513-576-6400
513-576-0022 (Fax)

Canadian
Distributor:

B. Broughton Company Limited
2105 Danforth Ave.
Toronto, Ontario
Canada M4C 1K1
416-690-4777
416-690-5357 (Fax)